"An incredibly inspiring and beautiful tale of a blessed journey of lessons learned as told through the voice of one man's (and humanity's) best friend, a loving dog named Barley. Ron Marasco transports both heart and mind heralding understanding and acceptance while weaving rich religious history within the pages of this unique adventure."

—KRISTIN CHENOWETH, TONY AND EMMY
AWARD-WINNING ACTRESS

"If you need a spirit-lift, a book of hope, a read that will urge you to believe that hope is worth the risk, you are holding the right book. Do yourself a favor—read and enjoy!"

—MAX LUCADO, *NEW YORK TIMES* BESTSELLING AUTHOR OF
GOD CAME NEAR AND *BEFORE AMEN*

"Some of the greatest life lessons about courage, loyalty, trust, and patience . . . I've learned from my dog. Read *The Dog Who Was There* and learn an amazing lesson about faith."

—ANDY ANDREWS, *NEW YORK TIMES* BESTSELLING AUTHOR OF
THE NOTICER AND *THE TRAVELER'S GIFT*

"*The Dog Who Was There* is a page-turning read that stops and opens the heart. Revealing profound truth with compelling grace, Ron Marasco offers a singular vision of the greatest story ever told."

—BETH HENLEY, PULITZER PRIZE-WINNING PLAYWRIGHT OF
CRIMES OF THE HEART AND *THE JACKSONIAN*

"*The Dog Who Was There* is a wonderful, engaging book that adds a completely new perspective to the Passion story. Ron Marasco has created a character in Barley who will entertain and inspire readers. The retelling of Christ's ministry through the human characters connects the reader in a unique way to the Gospel message, but it is Barley who will charm people of all ages."

—KEVIN BAXTER, ED.D., SUPERINTENDENT OF CATHOLIC SCHOOLS,
ARCHDIOCESE OF LOS ANGELES

The Dog Who Was There

The Dog Who Was There

RON MARASCO

THOMAS NELSON
Since 1798

Published in Nashville, Tennessee, by Thomas Nelson. Thomas Nelson is a registered trademark of HarperCollins Christian Publishing, Inc.

Thomas Nelson titles may be purchased in bulk for educational, business, fund-raising, or sales promotional use. For information, please e-mail SpecialMarkets@ThomasNelson.com.

Library of Congress Cataloging-in-Publication Data

Names: Marasco, Ron, author.
Title: The dog who was there / Ron Marasco.
Description: Nashville, Tennessee: Thomas Nelson, 2017.
Identifiers: LCCN 2016033039 | ISBN 9780718083922 (softcover)
Subjects: LCSH: Bible. New Testament—History of Biblical events—Fiction. |
    Human-animal relationships—Fiction. | Jesus Christ—Fiction. |
    Dogs—Fiction. | GSAFD: Christian fiction. | Bible fiction.
Classification: LCC PS3613.A7275 D64 2017 | DDC 813/.6—dc23 LC record
available at https://lccn.loc.gov/2016033039
Printed in the United States of America

17 18 19 20 21 RRD 5 4 3

To
Patricia Clarkson
whose gift for friendship
borders on the miraculous

"Truly I tell you," Jesus replied, "no one who has left home or brothers or sisters or mother or father or children or fields for me and the gospel will fail to receive a hundred times as much in this present age: homes, brothers, sisters, mothers, children and fields—along with persecutions—and in the age to come eternal life."

—MARK 10:29–30

CHAPTER 1

Barley was lying with his snout resting on the hearth, looking up with his alert brown eyes, watching Adah cook dinner. She was sitting, as she always did at this time of night, on her small stool and stirring a pot of something that, to Barley, smelled delicious. It was nightfall in the small home that Duv had built, all by himself, when he and Adah first became husband and wife, many years before Barley had come into their lives.

The walls of the homey, one-room house were thick, made out of light-colored stone and coarse mud, from the region of Judea they lived in, that Duv had sanded smooth with his own hands and had painted a peaceful shade of white. The stones had no sharp corners but curved softly, giving them a rounded feel that made the whole house look to Barley like the body of a jolly, well-fed person. The ceiling was low, which was a fine fit for Adah and Duv, since neither of them was very tall. The house had only one window—a large oval whose sill Barley loved to sprawl out on and look out onto the comings and goings of neighbors, goats, donkeys, and other assorted travelers on their way up the little road to the long thoroughfare that led to the marketplace or down it to the small pasture at the end of their street.

The whole house had a snug atmosphere that made Barley feel safe. He especially liked the comforting feel of this time of day—the lamp-lit, end-of-chores, dinner-cooking part of early nightfall.

It was at times like this that Barley felt life was good and that it always would be.

Whenever Barley got this feeling, he would roll his small body onto his back, allowing his scruffy off-white fur to push into the smooth hearthstone below him. Then he would raise his pink belly into the warm air of the room, let his paws dangle anywhere they wanted, and look up at the low ceiling and say to it with his eyes: *Ceiling, life is good, isn't it?* And he'd answer his own question by wagging his tail back and forth—quick as a sickle, swishy as a broom.

Tonight Barley's wagging was particularly enthusiastic because it had been a fine and fun day. It had been spent with his masters, Adah and Duv, doing chores that Barley found particularly interesting.

The morning, like most mornings, was spent watching Duv and Adah work in the tiny, well-tended front patch of land where they grew vegetables and had a large olive tree that always seemed full of thick, healthy olives that Barley liked to smell. On sunny days, like today, Barley always felt good-weather frisky. And when he felt this way, he would never leave Adah's or Duv's side in the garden, watching with great curiosity each new chore and even trying to lend his help. He'd often stick his tiny snout so close to what one of them was doing, he'd almost get conked on the nose with whatever tool they were using until they would say something like, "Do you mind, sir?" or "It's hard enough to weed without you licking my ear."

The second half of most days was the time Adah and Duv would each do their own work. And Barley would divide his time, being alongside one or the other of them throughout the rest of the day, each day, the seven happy years he'd lived with them. Today had been water day, so most of the afternoon was spent accompanying Adah as she carried the heavy, clay water jugs out of their house and down the path to the well in the middle of the neatly-kept dirt road that was shared by all the other little houses in their neighborhood—five or six in all.

Adah was an older woman, in her fifties—an old age for a woman in this place and time. She was rather short, and her body was somewhat plump in spots—which Barley liked, because it made her lap so comfortable he'd often hop up on it to watch her sew. Her hair was gray, her skin was soft and a little saggy in places, and her eyes were warm. When she smiled, Barley thought she looked as young and pretty as a little girl. But because she was old, some of her bones were stiff and unsure, so she moved slowly and carefully. Adah was not afraid of the hard work it took to keep a house well run in the first century AD on a humble street on the outskirts of Roman-occupied Jerusalem—even if the chore of the day was something strenuous like lugging water jars to the well, as it had been today.

Barley had been taught that, when accompanying her on this task, he should not walk within the usual petting distance, right near Adah's feet. It was fine to stay that close during all the other chores, and he would gladly accept the little pats she'd give him every few minutes or so—stopping her cooking or sewing or washing to lean down and give him a quick rub and a "Hi there, you" or "Good boy." But Barley knew he had to take special care on water-carrying days not to be too close when he walked with her. That way he'd never accidentally trip her as she hauled the heavy, brimming water jars back and forth between the well and their house.

It had almost happened once, a few years back, but they escaped with just a cracked jug and with water all over them both, which Duv, when he looked out the window and saw them, found funny. After that day, Barley had been trained to be cautious. He was small enough—between twenty and twenty-five runty pounds and less than a foot and a half high—that you could miss seeing him underfoot, though he was agile enough never to get stomped on. Usually Duv only had to correct him once before Barley understood, and Barley's affection for Duv made it easy to comply with the few rules that Duv patiently taught him. In all the years they had been together, Adah had never heard her husband raise his voice, a characteristic she attributed to the fact that she'd married a man "whose name rhymes with *love*."

The main rule Adah insisted on was that Barley never bite.

"A good dog doesn't bite," she said.

Barley liked watching Adah and Duv work. But he also understood that dogs have their chores to do, just as people do. His job was chasing birds in the yard—even though he was never able to catch any—and being petted, and being good company, and keeping the people he loved safe by watching over their tiny house and barking to let Adah and Duv know when a visitor came up the narrow path to their door.

Of all the little family's chores and rituals, it was Duv's job that seemed to Barley the most interesting of all. Duv did wood carvings—intricate little sculptures that were, to all who saw them, nothing short of lovely. That's why Adah disliked it when people in the marketplace called Duv a woodcarver. These little creations were so beautiful that to call Duv a woodcarver would, in the famous words of Adah, be "like calling God a world-monger."

Figurines was what he and Adah called them. And once a week, on Friday morning, when everyone in town was busy shopping for the evening's Sabbath meal, Duv and Adah would take the beautiful little figurines he sculpted from wood to the busy marketplace on the far side of their region and sell them.

These figurines were always of the same subject.

Birds.

But because Duv worked so hard to make each one of his wooden birds a special work of art, customers in the marketplace willingly parted with their coins to buy the charming trinkets. Duv was so good at what he did that he and Adah usually sold every figurine and would return with a coin pouch filled enough to get the three of them comfortably through the week.

Duv's small workbench was in the back corner of the low-ceilinged house. And Barley would watch as Duv worked there, for hours each afternoon and evening, diligently carving with his sharp, homemade tools into little blocks of wood the treasures that made him known, jokingly, by the neighbors on his street as the Bird Rabbi. Barley loved observing Duv as he sat hunched over a small piece of wood, his sun-weathered face down close to whatever detail he was expertly carving, occasionally blowing away the little curls of wood he'd shave off, which Barley loved to watch flutter to the ground like even tinier little birds.

Bit by bit, Duv would turn each piece of wood into the shape of a beautiful bird, every one in a unique pose. Then he would use an array of small twigs, the ends of which he had frayed with a tiny knife and made into brushes, to color his creations. Barley loved seeing Duv dip the different brushes into pots of interesting colors that Adah made for paint, using things like blackberries and crushed lily pollen and various plants she squeezed to drip out their pretty juice.

Even though Duv was strong for a man of his height, and had big hands and thick fingers, when he worked on the figurines—carving delicately, painting them gently—he put such lifelike detail into the sculptures, making the birds seem so *real* to Barley that, one day, the most astonishing thing happened.

Duv had just put the finishing touches on a figurine he'd worked at all day. Barley was lying by the fire next to Adah as she stirred the pot of dinner. He glanced across the room at the freshly painted bird sitting on Duv's workbench—a bluebird figurine with an orange beak and shiny, dark-green eyes. Suddenly, as Barley was looking up at the sculpture lazily, the bird turned its head, stared right at Barley, and winked!

Barley stood up and began to stare at the bird, to bark and bark at it until, finally, the bird winked at Barley one last time, turned its head away, and went back to being just a piece of painted wood drying on the workbench. Duv and Adah enjoyed Barley's reaction to the figurine very much. Adah even chuckled to her husband and said, "It's a compliment to your work, dear." Barley didn't know what this meant, but he never wanted to see one of the birds on Duv's workbench do that again. And, thankfully, none ever did.

Barley could tell by how carefully Adah and Duv handled the figurines that they were fragile and important. Duv even made a special basket in which to carry them during their long journey on foot to the marketplace. Duv always filled the basket with a heaping pile of fresh straw, and the birds certainly had a comfortable journey as Duv and Adah carried the basket—each holding a handle—a family of Duv's lovely creations nesting between them. And along the way to the marketplace, Adah would hum little songs. "My wife is a hummer," Duv would say to people about her, smiling.

On one side of the bird basket was a large wooden handle. That was the side Duv held on to when they carried it to market. On the other side was a smaller handle that Duv had carved and smoothed perfectly to fit Adah's smaller hand. And Barley had watched Duv work for two whole nights to craft a round lid for the basket that fit onto it perfectly. It was made from thin cedarwood, and around the perimeter, Duv had carved the words of an old prayer he loved, measuring perfectly so the last letter of the last word came back around to meet the first letter of the first word.

I will fear no evil, for you are with me.

And if that wasn't enough, he cut into the lid several precisely rounded holes. When Adah asked what the holes were for, Duv quietly answered in his usual matter-of-fact tone, "So the birds can breathe."

Tomorrow was a market day, so Duv was still daubing a final little flourish of color on the last bird of the week. Tonight dinner was looking as though it might be a little later than usual—even though Barley was by the hearth, waiting for the best moment of the day, when Adah would reach up to the shelf for Barley's wooden dinner bowl. On nights like this, when dinner was delayed, Barley would often doze off, breathing in the smell of the cooking meal between each peaceful snore.

Some nights, just before dinnertime, Duv would get up from his workbench and join Adah by the fire, and the two of them would pet Barley lightly at the same time, trying not to wake him. Which made Barley wonder if petting a dog together was how old people kiss, though Duv would sometimes kiss Adah anyway.

And some nights, as Barley drowsed, the fire in the hearth would paint moving images and shadows on the walls of the room, and when Barley closed his eyes to doze in their flickering light, soon his memories would paint their own pictures on the walls of his snoozing mind and Barley would have dreams—dreams that were vivid, real, and exact.

Tonight the dream began with an image.

Over seven years ago, when Barley was first born, he was lying in the sun next to his mother . . .

This was Barley's very first memory, in the earliest days of his life. The dream began with the memory of the afternoon sun moving across the field all morning till it finally came to shine on Barley and the other pups as they lay in the curve of their mother's belly. A week before, Barley's mother had given birth to a happy, squirming litter of puppies, the smallest of which was Barley.

Most of those early weeks of life had been spent lolling happily in a small clearing amid acres of crops and high grass that was their home. The clearing was on the farthest end of a landowner's large field along a rarely traveled stretch of swaying wildflowers and reeds. There, amid a thicket of low bushes, the property abruptly ended at the bank of a wide, fast-moving stream. This stream filled the field, day and night, with a constant gushing *whoosh*, and flowed for miles and miles through this region of Judea. The area was alive with birds, all variety of wild foliage, as well as other splendid sights for a new dog to see.

Barley and his siblings would spend the day looking up at the blue sky, which was how he first got introduced to butterflies—which Barley was very anxious to begin chasing as soon as his wobbly new legs were ready. By the end of most of those early days, when the sun sank below the line of the grass up above the small protected clearing, the family was ready for a well-earned night's sleep.

Even though Barley would feel tired, the darkness at night would scare him and keep him awake. Barley was the smallest pup in his family, the runt of the litter, and on nights when he was fearful, his mother would lower her comforting brown eyes to watch over him in the moonlight, and sometimes lean her head down to lick her small son's tiny snout. And Barley would press his head deep into his mother's soft belly. Barley noticed that when he pressed his tiny triangular ear into his mother's chest, he could hear coming from deep inside of her a kind of music, a gentle beating—*bum-BUM, bum-BUM, bum-BUM*—that let Barley know that, even when his mother was asleep, she was still taking care of him.

Since the part of the dream Barley was having as he lay by the hearth at Adah's feet was happy, he began to wag his tail, even though he was sound asleep. Soon Barley's dream wound its way to the memory of the very first friend Barley ever had. No one had made little Barley's tail wag as much as he could.

Micah . . .

B arley was only a couple of weeks old, but his eyes were now fully open and happily taking in all the new sights. And his tiny legs had grown strong enough that he could amble to the edge of the clearing to spend part of each day looking out at the waiting world beyond. One morning he was peering out through the tall grass at the rolling acres that ran along the nearby stream when he saw a sight that made him realize there were more creatures in the world than just dogs, butterflies, birds—there were other creatures that were far larger and more interesting that he had yet to meet.

Walking straight toward him was the boy he would come to know as Micah.

Micah was thin and small for his ten years, with dark brown hair and eyes so clear and green Barley could see their color even at a distance.

When Barley first saw him, Micah was carrying a huge basket, twice his size and tied to the boy's back with coarse rope that made ruts in his slight shoulders. The basket was filled with the firewood that Micah's father made him gather and carry. His father didn't need the firewood. The man was a wealthy farmer with a small army of farm laborers at his disposal. But Micah's father forced the boy to do things for reasons his young son didn't understand—or understood to be wrong.

Micah tried to sit down on the ground and rest a moment, but as he tried to pull his arms from the rope, the weight of the basket pulled him over. As he struggled to get free of the basket, he said with a burst of frustrated emotion, "This is so-so-so heavy. I can't do it . . ."

As Barley watched and listened, Micah plunked himself

down on his backside in the grass. Once there, the boy put his soiled cheeks into his hands and—believing he was alone and completely unaware that a two-week-old dog was inches away watching his every move—began to cry. As his slender body heaved up and down, he burst forth with sobs as hard and high as a ten-year-old boy can cry when something is breaking him.

Seeing and hearing this, Barley's young heart stirred. Before he knew it, Barley had reached out to the boy by means of an audible *yip* that was so loud and clear even Barley was surprised when it came out of his miniature mouth.

"Huh?" Micah gasped. The boy froze and held his breath in silence until Barley let loose with another sound. Micah's eyes lit up through his tears, and within a second he'd pulled himself up off the ground, ran to where the noises had come from, and pushed his head through the brush.

As soon as Barley lifted his tiny head and looked up into Micah's eyes, he saw how glad this small boy was to see him and understood how good it was to have someone be glad to see you. That's when Barley learned what friendship was— the feeling that you have always known someone, even if you've never met them before, mixed in with the feeling that you want to keep on knowing them forever.

Micah stepped cautiously into the clearing. Having

been raised on a farm, he knew to approach a pup only if the mother was calm. But seeing only his shining eyes and trusting, tearstained face, Barley's mother reacted to Micah no more than she would to a warm breeze blowing by. Seeing this, Micah bent down and gingerly reached for the dog who had called out to him, the pup with his head poking up from the pile of his soundly sleeping siblings.

"Hi there," Micah said as he scooped Barley up and cradled him against his chest.

"So little," he whispered. And pushing his face down to Barley's snout said of the small black nose, "Like a tiny fig," and he laughed.

It was the first time Barley had heard a laugh. And he liked it.

"Maybe you can be mine," Micah said in the tone boys use to share fun plans.

And from then on, Barley was.

From that first day in the field when they met, Micah visited Barley and his family every spare second he could be away from his chores. And each time the boy came to see them, he would bring Barley and his family new and wonderful presents. One day Micah arrived with a huge sack of straw and a piece of thick cloth to lay over it. This meant that Barley and his mother and siblings could be up off the hard ground at night when they slept.

Years later, after these happy days in the field had been taken away from him, Barley would remember the straw Micah brought for them when Barley watched Adah and Duv put the same soft straw in their basket to be kind to the wooden birds. But the gifts young Micah brought for Barley and his family went well beyond straw. There was the food! Every single day he would bring Barley's mother something to eat, like large chunks of fresh bread and chopped-up pieces of tasty meat, which Barley loved watching Micah feed to his always-hungry mother.

Micah and Barley would spend lazy afternoons lying face-to-face in the grass. Sometimes Micah would pluck a blade of grass to tickle Barley's snout, tracing it around the splotch of pink on his nose. On some days, Micah and Barley's happy visits would come to an abrupt halt.

"Micah!"

The voice would ring out low and loud from faraway.

"Your father is looking for you!"

Barley could see the boy's body tense, and Micah's face would lose its joy.

"Shhh," Micah would say, pressing his finger to his lips, and then with a quick head pat and a whisper, "Don't worry, I'll be back." And Micah would run away.

Even though Barley would miss Micah when he was away, Barley knew that the longer Micah was away, the happier they were to see each other. Barley would hear his friend come running and would begin wagging his tiny tail like mad as Micah's fast stride crunched through the coarse grass, every ounce of his bursting ten-year-old joy carrying him back to see his tiny friend.

Once Micah burst into the clearing, he always went first and right away to Barley. The boy would fall to his knees and gently push his face right into Barley's snout and let Barley's minuscule tongue give him a riot of wet licks up and down Micah's giggling face—from chin, to cheeks, even to eyelids.

"Are you mine?" Micah would ask and answer his own question with a "Yes, you are!"

Then Micah would start to use his dog voice, a special, squeaky, gritted-teeth voice that Barley loved so much that he would jump up onto Micah and they would both fall back into the high grass, laughing and rolling.

If only the dream stopped there, with images of sunny days and the sound of a young boy's joy.

But sometimes, even with Adah and Duv so near and the hearth warm and the dinner simmering, Barley's sleep would carry him away on a cold stream of the first terrible memories from his early life. For dogs, no less than for people, firsts matter. They echo long past their point in time, especially in dreams. It's true of the good firsts, and very true of the bad ones. That's why when a dog cries in a dream—even a full-grown dog, even an old dog—the cry it cries is the cry of a pup, because that's what it is doing when it sleeps—reliving a first.

CHAPTER 2

Barley had just had a fine meal and was relaxing in the sun, happily pressed up against his mother's belly, listening to the reassuring *bum-BUM, bum-BUM, bum-BUM* of her body.

Then, as Barley lay there, something new happened.

The comforting *bum-BUM, bum-BUM* rhythm inside of his mother got faster and faster.

Barley lifted his head from her chest to look up at his mother's face. As he did, he saw her tilt her head up and lift her ears tautly. She became very still. She was listening. And Barley could see that what she heard worried her.

Barley listened as well.

He could hear creatures across the field.

They were running. And they were getting closer.

This made Barley happy, as he loved the one visitor they'd had. He looked over to his mother to see if she was also happy, but as soon as his eyes fell on her, Barley saw that she was not only unhappy—she was frightened. His mother stood up so quickly that one of Barley's brothers fell from her nipple and plopped to the ground.

Barley watched his mother standing stiff and alert while his siblings lolled blissfully on the straw.

In that moment, Barley had his first awareness of what it meant to be a certain kind of son.

He knew he was going to have to be the one to help his mother. As Barley watched her pace back and forth, lifting her head to the field beyond, Barley looked up as well and peered through the little crevices in the high grass where he could already see far-off movement.

Barley's little legs had been getting steadier by the day, and now he put them to the test, scampering forward to the edge of the clearing where the tall grass began. Then he pushed his snout between two tufts and peered across the field.

There he saw three very large people running in the direction of his family's clearing. One man was tall and confident and wore a clean tunic. The other two men wore short worker's robes and thick sandals. Both of these men were so huge that at first Barley thought they were hills instead of people, until the two hills began running off in different directions.

As they parted, Barley saw someone else behind them, running as fast as he could to keep up with the three men. As soon as he saw who it was, Barley began to wag his tail.

It was Micah.

But as he heard him speak, Barley knew something was wrong.

"Nooo! Please, Father! Don't!"

Barley could feel his soft fur stiffen into cold spikes along his spine.

The man's voice was curt as he talked to the workers. "You brought the sacks?"

"Yes, we did, my lord."

"Follow me, you idiots."

This was the voice of Micah's father.

As the men drew near, Barley got a closer look at Micah's father. His cloak was neat and new. His black hair was thick and full and surrounded his face in a way that drew out the dark from his brown eyes. His pupils looked like two deep holes that were empty of any warm feeling, unlike Micah's eyes—which were, at this moment, looking up at his father.

"Father! Please!" Micah begged.

But his Father snapped back, "I'll give you 'Please!'

Where are they?" The man's voice echoed with its own authority. "Tell me or I'll flog you!"

Barley watched as the father grabbed Micah by the back of his tunic and pulled him along. Micah—still crying—struggled to keep from falling. Then the father pushed Micah out in front of him a few paces and pushed his leather-sandaled foot into Micah's backside, giving him a mighty kick that sent the boy reeling toward where Barley was crouched, watching them.

The father yelled to the workers, who were scanning the brush in search of something. "Over that way, you fools! Not by the stream!"

As the father drew closer, the man began screaming at his son with a bloodcurdling wrath that felt to Barley like it could break his small ears in half.

"I'll show you what happens when you don't do your chores! I'll show you what happens when you waste time playing with filthy mongrels!"

Barley finally heard the boy speak, and the quavering fear of his young voice made Barley hurt.

"Father, I am sorry! Please! Please don't. I'll do my chores! I won't play with them again!"

But nothing Micah said could stop his father's rage.

"You're a sneaky little thief! I'll show you what happens to any son of mine who steals food to waste it on useless curs."

By now Barley had seen enough to know his mother was right to be worried. He pulled his tiny head from between the grass and turned back to his mother. Her body stiffened, and she stood perfectly still. She pressed her strong paws into the dirt, her legs poised and ready. Then she tensed her face in a way that hardened her soft kindness into a strength that made Barley feel proud of her.

Instinct had made Barley's mother turn her back to the litter and do a head count. Not seeing Barley there, she looked around frantically. When she saw him a few feet away from the rest of the litter, at the edge of the clearing, she gave him a look that told Barley what she wanted him to do. He scampered behind his mother, standing at her back paws, in front of his huddled siblings.

"Here, sir! Over here!" one of the workers shouted to Micah's father. "They're over here!"

Within moments, the high grass circling the clearing was shaking violently. As soon as she saw the brush move, Barley's mother began a steady battle cry of noble barks. Then an enormous shadow suddenly darkened Barley's world as he looked up to see every bit of sunlight obscured by the arrival of one of the workers.

"Sir, I found them!" The man's voice boomed, and birds fled from nearby trees.

As his mother kept up the defensive pitch of her barks,

Barley saw that the worker was holding a large harvesting sack.

Moments later Micah's father, panting and red-faced, arrived in the clearing. He froze with rage when he looked down and saw the litter of dogs that had been living in his field.

The father was also holding a sack.

Then, as the two men glared down at the dogs, Barley heard Micah's voice. "Father, please don't hurt them! Please! Pleeeease!"

The boy burst through the clearing. He fell onto the ground at his father's feet a few inches away from Barley's mother, who was barking frantically. Micah grabbed hold of his father's leg, pressed his face into his thigh, and begged, "Leave them be, Father! They're my friends!"

But his father was having none of it.

"I'll 'my friend' you right over my knee as soon as I'm done with this one, you daydreaming little sneak!"

"Father . . ."

"Get away!" the man hollered, scraping the boy's face off his leg and pushing him to the ground.

This small flash of violence made Barley's mother bark with even more intensity.

Now the father began moving toward Barley's mother, swinging the heavy sack back and forth as he neared, whipping the air with the sack to frighten her. But Barley watched as his mother stood her ground, protecting her litter and giving her scrappiest son a first lesson in bravery.

The father leered at Barley's mother, leaned his head back toward the larger of the two workers, and ordered, "Go get me a stick or a rock!"

Barley's mother crouched slightly, readying herself to strike.

"No need, sir," the worker said, smiling. And before Barley's mother could lunge at Micah's father, the large man lifted his tree-size leg and kicked Barley's mother in the snout.

"Stop!" yelled Micah.

Barley watched as his mother reeled backward and fell onto her side—her growl evolving to a single high-pitched cry. Barley could see his mother was stunned and hurt. She tried to roll off of her back and right herself, struggling to stand up. But she was still dazed, so one paw went out from under her and she faltered onto three legs, wobbling.

Micah's father pointed to the weakened mother and told the worker who had kicked her, "You handle that one!" Then the father walked toward Barley and his siblings, snapping open the sack he was holding as he neared.

Micah tried again to reason with his father and said, "Father, punish me—but leave them be!"

"Don't worry, I'll punish you later. But first I'll handle these wretched creatures."

Micah's face turned ashen as his father signaled one of the workers to take the boy away. As Barley watched, peering up sadly, the worker wrapped his giant arm around the boy's thin middle and hauled Micah from the clearing, Micah pleading loudly with his father all the while.

A series of tiny anguished whelps could be heard from the clearing as Micah's father plucked up pup after pup and plopped them into the sack. Micah, seated on a rock where the brutish worker had placed him, watched from afar as his father wiped sweat from his brow and the other worker arrived with a thin piece of leather to tie off the sack. When Micah saw this nauseating sight, his heart sank and he lowered his head to let the tears pour forth.

And when he did, he found that he was looking down at a surprising sight.

Barley was at Micah's feet, staring up at him.

Micah let out a gasp of joy and admiration. The plucky little dog had slipped past Micah's father and managed to make his way to his young master's side. Micah bent down, dizzy with glee, and Barley hopped into his open arms. Then he drew Barley in close, hunching his shoulders around his dog as Barley licked his face.

"Give him here, sneak!"

It was the booming voice of the worker approaching. A massive hand reached down between boy and dog and wrenched Barley from Micah's arms with such force that Micah knew that if he did not let go of Barley, the brutal man's tug would rip the pup in half.

So Micah let go.

As Barley was carried away, he saw his first friend crumple into the grass, sobbing inconsolably.

The worker handed Barley off to Micah's father, who grabbed Barley's scruff.

"Idiots!" the father said to the workers. "You missed *this* one!"

The worker holding the closed sack pointed at Barley and said, "That one's the runt, my lord. The rat-catcher will have no use for him."

"That's true," the father said. "Hand me another sack and go find me a large rock. We'll drown him."

All the while, Barley hung from his scruff, caught in the father's vise grip. When Micah's father turned to see what was keeping the worker with the sack, Barley's vantage point shifted, and his eyes came to rest on his mother.

She was on the ground, with the other worker pressing his knee down on her to keep her still, her snout tied shut by a piece of leather and her eyes wide with terror. And then the men shared a laugh that men sometimes do when they're being mean.

In that moment, Barley matured a lifetime.

Barley watched as the large worker wrapped his massive arm around his mother's body, collaring her tightly and lifting her off the ground as she struggled to get free. Then, with his other arm, the man whipped the sack he was holding till the opening parted, and in one wrenching motion the man folded Barley's mother—hind legs first—into the open sack, leaving only her head peeking out through the opening.

She lifted her eyes and looked over at Barley.

He stared back at her and began to cry, making thin, whistle-like whimpers.

Barley saw his mother's face and could hear what she was now telling him with her eyes.

"We have to say good-bye now."

As Barley looked at her, her eyes said many things. They said love and sadness and hope, and all the things a mother could tell her son with a final glance. But they also said one more thing.

They said, *"I want you to live."*

Barley was determined to obey his mother.

The instinct rose up from deep inside of him and coursed throughout his tiny body, and before he even knew what he had done . . .

Chomp!

Barley had swiveled his head, lowered it onto one of the father's long fingers, and bit. The sudden pain made the man open his grip. The second he did, Barley squirmed out of his fingers and dove for the ground.

As he did, the worker reached down to grab the airborne pup but fumbled the large rock he was holding. The rock dropped squarely onto the sandaled toe of Micah's father just as Barley hit the ground and ran.

"Ahhhh! My foot—you idiot!"

Micah's father yelped and hopped around in pain ridiculously. Barley tried to speed away, moving his little legs as fast as they would carry him. But he could not outrun Micah's father, whose long strides were each equal to twenty of Barley's. Barley realized that running alone was not going to save him. So he looked inside himself for yet another instinct that might allow him to save himself.

Barley bolted in one direction until the father reached that way. Then Barley would halt and, quick as a blink, run in the opposite direction. Then the father would reach that way and, using the same trick, Barley would dart in the opposite direction, each time slipping through the frustrated man's grasp.

All this racing and darting only made the father angrier and more determined. But just as the raging man was redoubling his efforts to grab the scrambling pup, Barley saw a tiny opening under a perimeter of high swaying reeds. Fast as he could, he fled toward that opening and used his head and paws to push his way into the safety of spiky foliage.

As Barley burrowed his way through the tufts of leaves, his soft fur picked up all manner of spurs and nettles and seeds and buds and leaves and dirt. Barley squirmed forward as fast as he could, farther and farther into the thick foliage. Then he looked up and saw a sight that thrilled him.

Ahead, where sunlight was coming through an opening in the brush, Barley could see a long field of grass with mountains behind it. Barley ran with all his strength toward the field, knowing if he could get there, he would be free.

But then, midstride, Barley's eyes and ears both told him, *"Stop!"*

And he skidded in the grass, coming to a stop at the top of a steep embankment with a stream flowing down below, where Barley could hear the fast-moving *whoosh* of deep, dangerous water. The stream stood between Barley and freedom.

Barley quickly resolved to turn around and head back to the high grass that had previously sheltered him. But as he turned and prepared to hurl himself headlong into the brush—*whap!* He suddenly hit something hard, running into it full speed, and the impact sent an aching thud through his entire body.

It was the gigantic leg and sandaled foot of the large worker.

Dazed, Barley looked up to see a massive hand coming toward him. Soon he was hoisted into the air and turned around until he could see Micah's father running toward him, wildly shaking the empty sack. The man's face was twisted with rage, his cheeks scarlet, his eyes black—a nightmare charging straight at Barley.

The father opened the sack and made short work of dropping Barley into it. He did not even bother with weighing it down, as the other worker was still several yards back, running with a rock. The father simply wanted to be done with the whole aggravating episode.

As his tiny body crumpled down into the deep bottom of the sack, Barley began to cry. Lumped in a small ball, Barley looked back up at the man's face with the sun's rays behind him, beaming down on his thick black hair, making his face look like a dark cloud with eyes.

Then, in one sudden second, Barley was in total darkness. He could hear and feel the man tying the top of the sack as quickly and tightly as possible.

And as soon as the man was done, Barley could feel his body flip against the side of the sack as it made a high, dizzying arc through the air, landing with a splash. Barley could feel a floor of terrible cold beneath him that made him shiver in the blackness. And the cold and the dark made the silence inside the bag feel to Barley like he was alone in the universe. All Barley could hear was the sound of his own soft panting and the rushing of the water outside.

Until—very faint at first—Barley heard another sound.

A whisper.

Quiet at first, then more audible, and soon filling the sack.

He began to recognize the sound.

A voice.

A voice saying, sweetly, over and over: "I'm here . . . I'm here . . . I'm here . . ."

CHAPTER 3

I'm here!"

"I'm here, Barley. Wake up, boy."

Adah's voice was singsong tender but also strong.

"I'm here, little one. It's just one of your bad dreams."

Adah knew Barley's bad dreams often came if he dozed back off after the tail-wagging happy ones.

"I'm here, pet. Adah's here."

And she was.

This was not the first time Barley had had a bad dream. In fact, it was a fairly regular occurrence. And each time it happened, Adah would always stop whatever chore she was doing and go to Barley to reassure him, to let him know all was well, that she and Duv were there, by his side, and he had nothing to fear. Barley opened his eyes with a start and looked around blinkingly to reorient himself. It took him a moment to realize that it had been over seven years since the awful day he had dreamed of. And soon his little body eased into the understanding that he was here, safe, with the aroma of dinner filling Adah and Duv's snug home where he lived with two people who loved him and had saved him from his nightmares.

Duv and Adah's dinner was almost ready, so that meant it was time for Adah to reach up to the small shelf above the hearth and take down the wooden bowl that Duv had carved for Barley when they first brought him into their home.

It was always the same meal, and it was Barley's favorite—a few spoonfuls of grain swimming in milk, along with chopped-up pieces of chicken gristle, and the whole thing topped off with a dollop of honey. Barley liked it so much that, some days, he'd wish for sundown to come quicker so he could get to eat it sooner. Adah set his brimming food bowl down on the hearth in front of the fire, and while she set the table for her and Duv's dinner, Barley ate his.

This had been the routine each night of his life since they brought him home. And Barley now ate contentedly from the wooden bowl into which Duv had carved his name.

Barley.

Adah and Duv had discovered what his name should be even before they knew he was to come home with them and be theirs.

It happened one afternoon about seven years ago . . .

Adah and Duv were out looking for the kind of wood Duv used to make his figurines. The place he had the best luck finding it was close to one of the large streams on the far side of town. It was a long walk to get there but worth it, because as Duv always said, "The tree already has the sculpture inside—all I do is find it." So the choice of wood was important.

On this particular afternoon, he and Adah had just found a terrific piece of wood—one of the best in weeks—when they heard an odd sound.

Duv followed the sound through the trees and reeds and riverbank grass as Adah kept pace with him every hurried step of the way. They looked down from the bank, and in a second, they knew where the sound was coming from. They saw a large waterlogged sack that had gotten caught in some low branches of a tree on the bank.

At this point, Barley had been inside the sodden sack for a number of hours and even more miles along the powerful stream's path through Judea. He had shivered the entire long journey from the icy stream water that had gradually soaked through the bottom few inches of the thick sack. But the sack had stayed afloat. Micah's father had been so fed up with chasing him that he dumped him in the sack with no rock and tied the top of it so quickly and with such temper that he had knotted the sack that was still full of air. Barley had peered around the sack, thinking of his mother, wanting her there with him so he wouldn't be alone in the wet dark, moving for miles at a dizzying speed—until it had all stopped, just a short time ago, with a very light bump.

And then stillness.

Barley moved his eyes around, wondering if the sudden stillness meant he was now dead. The frigid water had soaked him through, and he was shaking down to his tiny bones. He had no idea where he was.

Now all he could do was cry.

But even that didn't work well for him. The cold and sadness had stopped up his throat till he couldn't even do a very good job of crying. He was shivering so much that almost no sound came out of his weepy, scrunched face: just a few thin, airy, high-pitched puffs of sadness.

But it had been enough for Adah and Duv to hear him.

Duv took the longest, strongest branch he could find on the bank, reaching it down to try to fish the sack out of the water.

"I've almost got it."

"Hurry, Duv! Listen to the poor thing!"

"I'm trying, dear, I'm trying."

Adah said heart-wrenchingly, "Oh, Duv! Please!"

"I've almost . . . almost . . . Ah! Got it!"

With a jolt, Barley could feel the sack start to ride again. This time only a few feet.

Duv used the long branch he broke off to reach out and pull the rapidly deflating sack to the embankment of the stream. Then he brought the sack, hanging now like a sad flag, over to the sunny grass and gingerly laid it down on the ground. Duv tried to open the sack, but the knot was too tight, so Duv took his knife and carefully slit it.

Into Barley's dark world came a bright flash of light.

He looked up and found himself staring into the lively faces of Adah and Duv, smiling in amazement at what they had just discovered.

Barley was wildly pawing Duv's strong arm as Duv gently pulled him out of the sack. Immediately he handed the squirming handful to Adah. Duv knew that what this wee fellow was most in need of, at the moment, was a woman's touch. And sure enough, Adah drew the pup right to her full, warm chest and held him there tenderly until Barley reached up his minuscule snout and licked her softly wrinkled face. After he had calmed a bit, Adah lightly brushed him off and lovingly picked off all the burrs and debris from his sodden off-white fur. As she flicked a last wet kernel off her finger, she said, "Barley. Bits of barley all over the poor little thing."

Then, after a pause, she exclaimed, "Barley! That's his name!"

To which Duv said, "Adah, dear—we shouldn't give him a name unless we intend to keep him."

But from the moment they had looked into his eyes and seen the pup so thankful to meet them, they knew that Barley would stay with them. Married over thirty years, childless, a comfortable but sometimes too-quiet house—of course he would stay.

Adah put her head down next to Barley's and felt him press his tiny wet head onto her cheek. "Do you want to come home with us?" she asked, her lips now touching Barley's head. Then Duv, in a singsong voice as he reached out his hand to pet him lightly, "We would certainly like you to come home with us . . . *Barley*!"

Now that Barley had finished his dinner, Duv and Adah sat down at the table to begin theirs.

They began, as they always did, by sitting at the small table near the center of the room, lighting a small candle, and saying their evening prayer. Barley watched as Adah and Duv bowed their heads and held each other's hands across the table and murmured their words of thanks. He could tell—the way dogs sometimes can—that something different was happening at those sweetly solemn moments when he heard his two masters change the tone of their voices and focus intently in a way that made the importance of it all register clearly with Barley.

For years the evening prayer had been said only by Duv, as the man of the household. Every night it would be a little different, depending on whatever good bits of the day the couple was thankful for, or whatever troubles they or the folks they knew were undergoing and for which they prayed for help and better days. Though not a man of many words, Duv would speak with earnestness, thoughtfully and slowly as he tried to put his thoughts into more formal words than usual. The way he did this always made Adah smile, because Duv would do his best to pray by saying words like, "Dear God, we thanketh thou . . . because thou giveth plenty of firewood . . . to keep us from the cold at night . . ."

But that was back before they heard about the Teacher—the Teacher from Galilee whom many people in Judea had been talking about of late.

Ever since then, instead of Duv's usual prayer, they would bow their heads as always, but then both their voices joined together to say words. They were the exact same words every night, and their voices reciting in unison made a musical sound Barley liked. And some of the words they said would make his ears perk up. Like when they said the part about. *"Give us today our daily bread . . ."*

Bread!

Barley heard that word, because *bread* was often the sound Adah made right before she'd stop cooking dinner to toss him a small chunk of old bread, gone crunchy over time. A favorite treat.

Another word Barley would react to was *forgive*. Adah and Duv said it like it was a special word. It was a word in the prayer they repeated: *". . . and forgive us our debts, as we also have forgiven our debtors."*

Duv always squeezed Adah's hand at the very moment the word was uttered during the prayer, and a glow seemed to spread beyond the dinner table, all the way across the room, to touch Barley.

It had been that way with this word ever since the first time Barley heard it pass from Duv's lips.

One year ago.

Duv had been out in the garden and had spoken to one of their neighbors, a very nice widow from across the road named Yael—a small lady with soft white hair and a pretty face who was Adah's good friend. That morning Yael had been telling Duv all the things that were being said by the Teacher from Galilee.

When she spoke about him, Yael did so with a hushed voice, because some people disliked what the Teacher had been saying and thought he should be stopped. But she must have thought it was safe to talk about the Teacher in front of Barley, because Barley was lounging on the sunny window ledge as Duv and Yael sat chatting down below him in Duv's little garden.

That afternoon Barley was out with Duv, watching him tend to the plants in the garden, and Barley noticed that, time and again, Duv would stop his work and get lost in thought. And sometimes reach over and pet Barley, even longer and softer than usual.

Near sundown of that same day, Barley and Adah were walking back to the house from the small nearby patch of woods where they went to gather kindling. When they returned home, Duv was sitting in his chair waiting for them. He had something on his mind. He was excited in a way that was not normal for Duv.

"I spoke to Yael today."

"What?" Adah said, concerned for her friend. "Is she all right?"

"Oh yes, fine, Adah-la."

Adah-la was what Duv called his wife whenever he was feeling enthusiastic.

"She told me about a word. Just one word. So simple.

But it could change people. Change them, Adah-la. Like a miracle! That's the Teacher's idea. Forgiveness. That's the word! To *forgive* . . . wonderful, no?"

Adah listened intently but didn't seem to understand her husband.

"The word was such a blessing to me today, Adah-la. You can't imagine what I did . . ."

"What did you do?"

Duv told her about something that happened earlier that day between him and the man who lived across the street, next to Yael's house. This man was not a good person. His name was Hazor, and no one on their street trusted him. He was known for being polite to neighbors while talking to them and then being nasty about them behind their backs.

Adah was not fond of this man, and when she spoke of him—which was rare—she got a look on her face that was different than when Barley heard her talk about anyone else. This was understandable because, for one thing, Hazor was also given to petty thievery. He never stole anything that could get him into much trouble with the Roman soldiers who patrolled Judea, just small, everyday things that he could lay his sticky hands on when someone wasn't looking. He'd pluck a piece of fruit from a tree in a neighbor's garden as he passed, for example. And, if caught, he'd say the fruit had fallen in his path. Often he would walk across the street to Adah and Duv's front yard to talk to Duv as Duv worked. Hazor would say, "Duv, my friend, it's been so long since I've said hello!" Afterward they'd notice that their pile of wood by the front door was short a log. Adah used to say, "A hello from Hazor means good-bye to some firewood!"

But all that was before that day.

"Today, dear," Duv went on excitedly, "I was working at my bench and saw a head sneaking slowly by the window. It was Hazor, tiptoeing up to steal some of our logs. I think he knew you were out gathering wood and thought I wouldn't notice any missing from the pile with new logs coming. I think he's done that before."

"I'm sure he has," Adah interrupted, indignant.

"Usually this would have made me angry."

"I should hope so, Duv!"

"But then I thought of this word *forgive*. And like a kind of magic, I felt as if a heavy burden I had been carrying a long time had been lifted from me."

Adah was stunned. "Fine for you, Duv, but do you know the 'heavy burden' I've been carrying? Firewood! Lugging it all the way home for that man to pilfer! Listen to yourself—a 'heavy burden lifted.' Lifted indeed . . . lifted like our firewood was by that sneaky menace!"

"Adah. Oh, Adah-la. You won't believe what I did next."

"What?"

"I hope you won't be angry."

"Whaaaat?" Adah repeated, in that way a wife does when she knows her husband is about to tell her he did something stupid.

"I picked up the few logs he'd left us in the pile. I walked across the path to his house. I knocked on his door. He opened it. I walked in and handed him the logs and said, 'These are for you. I forgive you for everything you've stolen from us.'"

There was a pause. Then . . .

"Oh my word, Duv! What did his large wife say?"

"She screamed!"

"Duv, have you lost your mind?"

"Lost my mind? Yes, dear—but only the part of my mind that made me feel bad."

As Adah shook her head, Duv laughed and then began to give Barley a belly rub, which Duv did when he was in an especially good mood.

Adah was skeptical about the ideas of the Teacher at first, but Duv had a way of being very persuasive—as is true of husbands who don't talk very much. And soon Adah began to see for herself that thinking and talking about the words of this Teacher helped Duv. Not to be kinder—Duv was always kind—but to be more relaxed, to sleep better, to whistle more, and to smile with true satisfaction after he was done with one of his figurines, as opposed to just looking at it for the flaws in his paint strokes.

Once, Adah and Duv even went to hear the Teacher speak, traveling a day's distance to hear him. They had been so touched by all the wonderful things their neighbor Yael had recounted to them about the Teacher that Duv had worked for days to carve as a gift for him the prettiest figurine he'd ever made: a large bluebird perched on a rock, its wings spread slightly. This bluebird had beautifully expressive eyes that seemed to magically follow you no matter what angle you looked at it from—a feature that particularly amazed Barley.

On the day they traveled to hear the Teacher, they attempted to give it to him, but in the crush of the crowd they weren't able to get close enough. Then some very serious-looking soldiers and high priests came to find out what he had been saying, and all those important-looking men stared suspiciously at the crowd. Duv had been warned by Yael that it could be dangerous to let people know you were a follower. At one point, a pair of soldiers had turned sternly and looked directly at Duv.

It was the only time in their long marriage that Adah had seen her husband terrified.

But he was mainly terrified for her, until the soldiers—notorious for mistreatment of regular citizens, finally looked away.

"When the soldiers show up, Adah, bad things happen."

But Adah and Duv were never people to dwell on the bad things. So, unable to give the Teacher his gift of the bird, they simply brought the figurine back home and Duv put it on the small shelf over their bed, where at least, as they fell asleep under its wing, they would be inspired to think about the Teacher and his message.

Barley liked having the bird up there on the shelf. Often at night—especially after he'd have the bad dream—he'd wake up and look around to see if Adah and Duv were still awake, but then glance across the room at two comfy lumps under the blanket breathing in sync. On nights like that, when Barley was up alone, he liked looking up at the bird over their bed.

By now Adah and Duv had recited their dinner prayer together, murmuring softly in rays of candlelight as they held hands across their tiny table. Duv had worked especially hard this week, so there were even more bird figurines than usual to sell tomorrow at the market. But the more figurines to sell, the more work it took to show them off to the customers. This was usually Adah's job, because Duv was too shy to say nice things about his work. But not Adah!

On nights like this, before a market day, Adah and Duv went to bed early, right after they had dinner. Merchants—especially the humbler peddlers like Duv and Adah—went to the market before dawn to ensure they got a good spot to sell their wares. Because tomorrow evening was the start of the Sabbath, those who marketed tended to come early in the day so they could be home before sundown. Adah and Duv had to awaken while it was still dark outside to have time to carefully pack up the figurines and ready themselves for the journey up the long, winding road to the marketplace.

As Barley watched his masters finishing dinner, the house was filled with a sense of peace. Since the Teacher had come into their lives, the small house they lived in—which had always been a snug and happy place—became even more so. It was not so much that Adah and Duv had learned from the Teacher how to be kinder and happier and more appreciative of life. It was rather that the Teacher had put into beautiful and memorable words what this couple already knew to be true about how to live.

CHAPTER 4

Barley was a dog who normally liked to sleep late, but today being market day, he had gotten up very early. As soon as Adah awoke to start the fire when the sky was still dark, Barley roused himself and lay by the hearth with his snout on the ground, looking up and following with sleepy eyes all of the bustling activity of Duv and Adah readying for market.

After his morning walk with Duv, Barley came back in the house to be greeted by Adah, who had filled his bowl with plenty of water to get him through the day. After the usual series of market day rituals, including extra belly rubs and a few treats left over from dinner, Barley's masters were ready to make the journey up the long road to the marketplace.

Very carefully Adah and Duv picked up their basket, filled with a colorful flock of Duv's creations sitting contentedly on a nest of straw. And then they left for the day. Barley hopped, as usual, up onto his perch on the wide ledge of the window to watch his masters amble up the street and out of sight.

Most of the morning, Barley sat in the window, watching the activity on their small street. Since this was Friday, tonight was the special evening meal before tomorrow's Sabbath. Neighbors were up early to begin making preparations so they could be home before sundown—as was the custom in all pious households throughout Judea.

By midday Barley had finally found a sunbeam, which always made him happy, because Barley never had bad dreams when he slept in a sunbeam. And after taking a long drink of water, he curled up in its warmth, enjoying the quiet of his home and thinking about the meal he would have after Adah and Duv returned. In a moment, Barley was fast asleep.

He'd been like that for hours, but now, with the sun fading and a gloaming wind blowing through the window, Barley began to rouse himself. He yawned a few times and lay in the middle of the floor, content and rested.

The only bad thing was that he was feeling hungry.

Hungrier than usual.

Barley knew that being hungry would only make dinner taste better when he had it later, and that thought only made him happier. He rolled over onto his back to get into his usual happy pose: belly up, paws dangling, tail swishing the floor with intermittent wags.

But when he did, he caught sight of something that wasn't quite right.

It was the sky.

The sky was a certain shade of pink that Barley knew well—a pale grayish-pink color, the soft light of which eased all the day's cares.

It was the shade the sky always was when Barley took his evening walk with Duv—the special time he and Duv had alone together each night, when they'd walk to the small pasture at the end of the street and see Namm the goat and his owner coming up the other way to go home to their house.

It was the shade the sky always was when Duv would find a stick and toss it ahead so Barley could run and catch it. Barley would grab the stick in his mouth and rush back to Duv, and Duv would bend down and pet his head and say, "Barley boy, Barley boy, Barley boy!"

It was the shade the sky always was when they walked back to the house, able to smell Adah's dinner cooking as they approached.

It was the shade the sky always was when Adah and Duv were already back from market and the three of them were together after a day spent apart. Together for a happy evening.

But none of those things had happened yet, because Adah and Duv were not home.

On the day of the Sabbath meal, Adah and Duv were always home when the sun was still well up in the sky so that they had plenty of time to finish up the work of the day and keep the Sabbath as holy as it was meant to be kept.

Barley looked out into the road for someone to help him find Adah and Duv.

Across the road he could see Hazor in front of his house, drinking from a wineskin. Barley barked to get his attention, but Hazor was too busy drinking and mumbling to himself. Barley looked down onto the ground.

Should he jump?

Adah and Duv had trained him only to leave the house through the door and never to jump to the outside from the window ledge.

Barley had never disobeyed Adah and Duv, but now he faced a terrible dilemma as he stood on the wide window ledge, yearning to go find help—his paws at the rim of the ledge as he looked down and barked at the ground below. Some instinct was telling him, *Jump! Go get help!* But another instinct was telling him, *Obey! Stay!*

After a moment, the first voice won.

Barley leaped onto the ground below, then ran through their tiny front yard and across the street to Hazor's house. Barley stopped a few feet away from the man, looked up into Hazor's red eyes, and began to bark pleadingly.

Hazor sneered wearily, "Shoo, dog! Go!"

But this made Barley bark even more—to try to let Hazor know how much he needed his help.

Suddenly, the front door swung open and Hazor's enormous wife was there. "Quiet, you wretched beast," she yelled angrily. "Always making noise! It's the Sabbath, runt! Don't make me beat you." Then she picked up a large stick from their woodpile and tossed it hard at Barley. He could tell by the way the stick flew toward him that she did not want to play fetch.

Barley ran into the middle of the road.

He stood there looking around the small street and wondering what to do. Then he began moving in circles, continuing to bark, as Hazor and his wife yelled at him from their yard. The gray of dusk had taken over whatever pink had been in the sky, and the street was silent and empty.

Barley realized he would get no help from sticky-fingered Hazor or his gigantic wife, that he would have to be the one to help his masters.

He knew what he had to do.

He would try to follow Adah and Duv's scent as far up

the road as he could. It had been years since he had gone with Adah and Duv to the market when he was still a pup—too small to be left alone all day. That was over seven years ago, but Barley felt sure he remembered the way.

He sped to the top of their tiny road and began to gallop as fast as he could up to the bend where the road opened out to the wider street, the very bend where Barley had last seen his masters early this morning as they set out on their journey.

For the past seven years, Barley's world had consisted only of Adah and Duv's house, their short road, the few small houses that made up their humble, quiet neighborhood, and the pasture and forest surrounding their little corner of the world. Crowds, busy roads, journeys, strangers, unfamiliar sights, loud noises—none of these had been part of his life these past years.

He was scared about where he was going, but he had no hesitation.

He had to find Adah and Duv.

Barley journeyed the strange roads at a frantic pace, leaving familiar places far behind him. Eyes, ears, nose—every one of his senses was heightened and keen and working hard to find his masters.

He felt he could still smell their scent on the wind—so faint it may have been a wish, or his imagination, but it was enough to keep him running in that direction, running and running—running down the long road toward the marketplace.

Barley began seeing clusters of people walking down the road in the opposite direction, and he ran past them. These were townspeople arriving home late from the market, rushing home to be inside before sundown. Most of them looked as though they had put in a hard day of work, and none were smiling. The people who did not care about the Sabbath were of a notoriously shadier class than those who were home well before sundown. And some of the people he saw walking toward him seemed tougher than those who lived in his neighborhood.

Less pious, even, than Hazor.

Some of them seemed almost dangerous to Barley as he ran past them as fast as he could.

Barley knew he was far from home. The fading light, the unfamiliar people, the confusing twists in the landscape made Barley feel like he was running up the road of a bad dream. But he kept moving, pushing himself, racing uphill, sniffing, looking, listening, and hoping to catch the smell, sight, or sound of his beloved masters.

Barley followed the road over, around, and through its

many gradual inclines and downward slopes through the town. He had already traveled a long way and was becoming fearful he had somehow veered onto the wrong road. He considered the awful notion he might be running far and fast in a direction that was actually taking him farther from Adah and Duv rather than closer to them, all while precious minutes of remaining daylight were quickly disappearing.

As Barley rounded a bend in the road, he saw two men walking together toward him, each carrying a half-empty sack. Barley had seen these sorts of sacks carried by the merchants among whom Adah and Duv worked and lived, but Barley could tell by the tone of their voices that these two men were not people Adah and Duv would want to know. These merchants seemed nasty and hard, and both men had cruel laughs that Barley did not like. The men were coming down the road, having just walked away from some commotion farther on.

Barley soon saw what the commotion was. Two Roman soldiers were standing with a small group of citizens at the side of the road under a very large tree. Barley then saw the two soldiers walk away from the small crowd toward their horses.

To Barley, who had only ever seen the hardworking labor horses who trudged daily up and down Adah and Duv's street, these massive beasts—with their powerful haunches, flaring nostrils, clanking metal reins, and heavy hooves—were like impressive but frightful monsters. And if the animals themselves were not scary enough, the soldiers mounting them looked even more menacing. They wore heavy armor in large, ominous shapes and large boots made of leather and yet more metal. Heavy red capes hung from their beefy shoulders, and their massive helmets made them stand high as giants. The soldiers carried tall, heavy spears, with tips so sharp and shiny that Barley had to look away from their pointy threat.

Soldiers like these were one of the unfortunate facts of life for citizens living in Roman-occupied Judea. They policed with a heavy hand and an itching palm. Throughout the region, these men were known for their brutality, corruption, pillaging, and drunkenness—and above all for tormenting powerless citizens as a kind of sport. The punishment they meted out was always swift and often public, and they were indiscriminate in choosing their victims—sometimes riffraff and troublemakers but just as often poor citizens or common laborers and merchants who were unable, or unwilling, to oblige them with bribes.

Barley's every instinct told him that these men were to be feared. And the instant the soldiers dug their sharp spurs into the haunches of their steeds, his instincts were proven correct.

Thunder erupted! A rumble shook the ground until it rattled every bone in Barley's body, and he looked up the street to face the monsters heading right for him! The huge horses were charging right toward Barley, with not the slightest indication they would be adjusting their path to avoid squashing the small dog in the middle of the road.

Barley zigged expertly to one side. But as he did, he saw the horses readjust their path directly toward him. When Barley looked up at the faces of the oncoming soldiers, he understood why. The mirthful look in their eyes and the hateful smirks on their faces let Barley know that running down small dogs was something these men did for fun.

As the stampede roared down the street toward him, one of the merchants they were about to pass waved up at the soldiers enthusiastically. The soldiers veered from Barley toward the merchants, one of whom shouted jubilantly, "Fine work, strong sirs! Huzzah!" The soldiers gave them nods as they passed, high-stomached with conceit, and kicked up a gale of heavy street dust that pelted Barley's fur as they flew down the road.

Barley changed his mind about the two merchants. They were disreputable men, but they had saved him. He passed by the men and headed toward where the crowd was gathered under the tree.

"Listen to you," one merchant laughed, mocking his friend's fawning. "Fine work, strong sirs! You gull!"

"Shut up," his friend said. "You see what happens to people these monsters don't like."

"Hey," said the other man, no longer laughing. "Did you get a look at who it was they hanged?"

"Only saw a couple of bodies. Too squeamish to look much closer."

"They're hanging people for everything these days."

"And well they should," barked the man who had thanked the soldiers, "to keep us safe."

"It's not to keep us safe," the other merchant said. "It's to keep us quiet. More and more and more the Romans are spooked by troublemakers. They're not just hanging thugs and cutpurses—they're hanging rabble-rousers, even blasphemers."

"Good!"

"Like the people who follow that teacher from Galilee."

"Really?" said the man who cheered the soldiers. "My wife thinks that neighbor of ours is becoming a follower."

"Turn him in," his friend said maniacally.

"Not a bad idea! He monopolizes the well on our street. I'd love to see him hang!"

Barley's head swirled with uneasy thoughts, but nothing stopped his legs from propelling him toward the crowd to make sure that Adah and Duv were not there.

A cluster of about eight or so people were gathered around, looking down into the back of a horse-drawn cart.

It was a low, wooden-slatted conveyance pulled by a single gray nag. The driver of the cart had lost all of his teeth, but that didn't stop him from talking away in a loud and crackly voice. He seemed to enjoy having the attention of the passersby who had stopped to have a look at the inside of his long cart and to ask about the soldiers.

"That's the way of things," the old man laughed. "Roman justice! Soldiers roaming the streets looking for people to make an example of. And good they do, if you ask me."

Barley could now see what was in the cart. A wide piece of rough cloth was draped over a flattish mound of something lumpy and angular around which the citizens gathered, some laughing, some gasping, all staring at what was in the cart.

Barley got close enough to the crowd to confirm that Adah and Duv were not among the onlookers. Barley was on the verge of abandoning the street to explore another road when the wind shifted and he caught the telltale whiff.

On the dusky air, he'd caught it—the scent of Adah and Duv.

All of Barley's senses became alert. He began to sniff and wag his tail, prancing to and fro, until his eyes landed on a sight that stopped him. A lady in the crowd moved to get a better look at what was in the cart, so that now Barley also could see.

A man was lying in the back of the cart, his head covered with a large piece of rough cloth. The only part of him Barley could see with any detail were his feet, which hung over the edge of the cart and had on the same common work sandals most laborers and merchants wore. The man was very, very still, more still than Barley had ever seen a person, even sleeping.

Barley took a few steps closer to the cart to see if he could get a scent. As Barley neared, one of the citizens, a gray-haired man, yelled out excitedly, "What was the crime? Thievery, blasphemy? What?"

The driver answered the man with a laughing, enthusiastic flair, saying, "See for yourself!"

The driver reached down into the cart with a flourish and lifted the cloth off the man's face, and there he was for all to see.

His eyes open and all of him still as a stone.

Once Barley realized what he was looking at, his angle of vision shifted—and he felt the road beneath him kick up dust into his face. It was only then, when Barley's front paw had gone out from under him, that he knew how scared he had been that it might be Duv.

It wasn't.

The man was younger. But it was still a man. And in a condition Barley had never before witnessed. A rope was tied tightly to his neck, and the man's face was the color of sand, not the human pink Barley was used to. The end of the rope had been cut and was frayed and hanging limply out of the cart.

The cart driver laughed. "This one was a common thug." And he took a stick and pushed it into the man's face, grotesquely moving the body's otherwise motionless cheek.

Barley knew the soldiers had done something bad to this man who was lying so still in the cart with rope on his neck. The driver's loud, bragging tone and the crowd's ugly laughter filled the air with the sort of fast-traveling stink of human cruelty that Barley (like most animals) had a nose for.

Barley's nose also told him that Adah and Duv had been here. He was sure of it. The wind had become strong enough that when it blew past Barley's snout, it filled his sensitive nostrils with the sweet and familiar scent of Adah and Duv.

Before he had even finished inhaling their comforting scents, Barley heard the sound of people walking toward him up the hill from the marketplace. He knew Adah and Duv would be surprised to see him there, but also glad— because they always were when they saw him. He only hoped they would not be disappointed in him for having broken the no-jumping-out-the-window rule.

Barley stood at the crest of the hill waiting and wagging.

But the lady and man Barley saw cresting the hill were, to be certain, not Adah and Duv. In fact, this particular couple were about as far from Adah and Duv as they could get. They were loud and giggling foolishly, and both of them reeked of wine. They held on to each other as they staggered up the hill past Barley. They drunkenly surveyed the old horse, the ghoulish driver, and the body in the cart and exclaimed loudly, "Oh—too bad. We missed a hanging!"

"Yes, you did," the driver laughed. "A couple of soldiers bought this fellow a one-way trip to the boneyard, if you get my meaning!"

"So what did he do to get himself hung?"

"Killed two merchants coming up from market. An old couple. This thug came from behind that boulder, where he'd been hiding. Attacked them up there. Near where that little dog is sniffing around."

He had only taken a few steps toward the marketplace when he saw it.

Adah and Duv's basket, lying smashed in the street.

The straw that he had watched Adah and Duv place in the basket this morning to make the birds comfortable on their journey was strewn in the road. The handle—the larger one, the one on Duv's side—was hanging off limply, like the rest of the basket had been wrenched away from it. And a huge foot had stomped on the delicate cedar lid into which Duv had carved words, and it was smashed to pieces.

He looked at the basket. He sniffed it. Even nudged it once with his nose.

He knew.

Barley knew his masters were gone.

It was the way he felt their scent leaving on the desert wind that told him.

Barley knew he was alone in the world now.

As he stood in the street, looking down at their shattered basket and realizing his masters had left him behind, Barley hoped that wherever Adah and Duv had gone, the two of them were still together.

I will fear no evil, for you are with me.

CHAPTER 5

The sky was a deepening gray now, and darkness would come soon.

Nightfall had always meant one thing to Barley . . .

Dinner.

The wind had been blowing for hours, and now Barley felt its chill in his bones. He had not realized how cold and hungry he was when his every instinct was focused on finding the people to whom he belonged. But now that he belonged to no one, standing alone in the darkening street, nightfall had new meaning.

Cold.

Then Barley heard a sound that roused him.

Humming.

It was not the sort of humming Adah always did. This was a man humming. His ears flew up and he listened to the merry sound on the otherwise silent street. He could tell the man was drawing near, just about to come up over the hill.

And when he did, Barley was happy to see not just a man, but a woman too. This couple was much younger than Adah and Duv, but Barley could tell they were similar to his formers masters in how they matched. Except in this couple it was the man who did the humming.

Maybe they could be his new masters. Maybe they would give him dinner.

Barley wagged to greet them and waited for them to see him.

But as soon as the man noticed him, he stopped humming. Barley could tell by the look in their eyes that something was wrong. They were frightened of him.

Barley knew that desert dogs were something to be frightened of—the big, long-snouted, fierce-fanged creatures that roamed the night. But he wanted to assure this nice couple that he was not one of them. So he began to take a few tentative steps toward them. But as soon as he did, the woman let out such a nervous cry that Barley froze right away.

Then very calmly, so as not to alarm them, Barley lay down on the street and looked away from them. He knew this was best so they could pass by him as they continued down the road without being worried he would hurt them.

And that's what they did. They passed him and continued on down the road and out of sight.

Barley would have felt sad except that as soon as the couple left, he heard other voices coming from farther up the road. Voices that sounded high and happy.

Soon Barley found himself looking up at two young boys.

One was a tad older than the other, both around eleven or twelve years old, and they were walking along with their father, who looked to be some kind of laborer.

Barley immediately sent out one quick, bright bark.

The young boys' attention snapped to Barley. When they saw him, their faces bloomed into wide grins, and they ran down the street toward Barley, ogling him and giggling as they neared, as their father yelled out a few parental words of caution.

The sight of their smiling faces rushing to him made Barley wag his tail until his haunches danced and his tongue bobbed happily out of the side of his mouth.

After getting a good look at him, the two boys whispered something to each other. Then they looked up and down the street to see if this dog's owner might be anywhere nearby.

When they saw no one else, they looked back at Barley tentatively.

Barley tried wagging, pleading with his eyes.

The boys ran back over to their father, and whatever he said made the boys laugh.

The boys ran back toward Barley, stopping in the middle of the street about twenty yards away from where Barley stood. The boys both squatted down in the street. They were now at eye level with Barley and peered over at him with fascination.

Barley gave them a few cheery yaps in the hope they would come over. But instead, one of the boys tossed something toward Barley that flew over his head and landed in the thicket behind him.

Fetch? Barley wondered.

Barley was very tired but would certainly play some fetch if they wanted. He wagged his tail as he turned around to look at the street and see if he could find the stick. But he saw no stick in the street. So he turned back around to the boys.

As soon as he did, he saw a rock heading for his face. Barley ducked, just enough so that the flying rock missed his snout and only grazed his ear—but with a very sharp sting.

Then he looked over at the boys, wagging his tail

awkwardly and shaking his leg to flap away the pain smarting his ear and maybe even the terrible awareness of what two boys, who looked so friendly, had just done to him.

The boys began laughing excitedly and looking around for another rock to throw.

Barley barked—sharply but sadly—as he crouched, watching the boys' movements closely so he would be ready to fend off any other flying rocks.

But the father had let his boys have their fun, and now it was time to get home since it was already dark. The three of them made their way across the street and down the road and were soon out of sight.

Never in his life had Barley felt more alone.

Barley turned away from the empty marketplace and began to walk on the crossroad in front of it, up the long, barren street. And before he knew it he was actually running.

By now a thick darkness had covered his way. Barley looked around for another street to explore. He turned down a smaller road that wound around for a long way until he came to another road, and then another, and from there Barley trotted along that thin and twisty road with no idea where it would take him.

Barley continued to trot, then ran a little faster—then

faster and faster, until soon he was running much faster than a dog as hungry and cold as he was should. He couldn't help himself. Barley was now so hungry he found that the only way to stop thinking about his painfully empty belly was to run even faster.

And he kept at this until . . .

He smelled something in the air. Barley stopped and sniffed.

The smell was smoke. But the smoke had a bitter smell to it, and seemed to be mixed with other strong smells— smells that weren't entirely pleasant.

But when you are cold, even bitter-smelling smoke means there's warmth to be had. And soon Barley's sensitive nose had pointed his body in the direction of the smoke and the other curious smells.

Barley eventually rounded a slight curve in the road and saw flames in the distance. They were at the end of a long path that cut through some rocky terrain dotted with brush. Barley began walking up this sorry-looking little road, heading toward the flames, when he saw a sight he had never before seen.

Along the path was a series of tiny makeshift huts, no bigger than the length of a person. They were low to the ground, ragged, and filthy. As Barley passed by them, he could see that there were people in most of them—

tired-looking people huddling beneath their thin cloaks, some sleeping, some peering out and shaking with cold.

The end of the road was within Barley's sight, only about a few hundred yards away. And the smell of the fire was stronger, filling the dark night sky with plumes of dark smoke. As Barley continued toward the fire, he heard a sound rising up out of one of the small roadside huts and went to investigate.

A lady was lying inside of the shelter. Barley could see by the way she moved her lips that the noise he heard was her singing.

As he got even closer, he saw that the lady was lying next to a small person—so small Barley didn't even think it was a person, until it moved slightly. The lady was holding this tiny person up against her body.

The way the two of them were curled up together reminded Barley of his mother, and the way that he, as a puppy, had fit so perfectly in the curve of her belly.

Barley continued down the path toward the fire and soon came to the end of the small road, where he discovered a large opening in a dense thicket. The area Barley had stumbled upon was on the very outskirts of the city and covered a few acres, about the size of a small lake. He took small, tentative steps into the thorny vestibule of this eerie place and peered into the clearing beyond.

Quite a few people were gathered, huddled in small clusters of two, three, or four. Most were trying to warm themselves by fires of various sizes—some wildly ablaze, others barely glowing with pitifully smoldering embers— but all of them smelling bad and filling the air with the stench of a city's discards.

While the people here were of different shapes, sizes, and ages, they all looked dirtier than most people Barley had seen before. Most of them were unusually thin, and as a few of the older ones got up to walk, Barley saw that they had bent limbs, making their silhouettes look like small dead trees moving against the night sky.

A few men could be heard singing—one beautifully, one making a terrible babble. But most of the hollow-looking inhabitants of this place merely sat mutely as they stared into their fires. Occasionally, Barley could hear the air fill with a raucous laugh or an angry outburst.

The inhabitants of this place called it the camp. To the rest of the civilized city of Jerusalem, the place was a notorious no-man's-land filled with the poor, the disenfranchised, the diseased—all unwelcome in the city itself, especially under the strict governance of Judea's Roman occupiers. But the isolation and infamy of the camp was a kind of refuge for its inhabitants. This area was the one part of Judea where the downtrodden and displaced could avoid being roughed up by the soldiers who policed the rest of the city. In the government's estimation, there was no one in this part of town worth protecting, so it was one of the only places of true freedom in all of Judea.

Barley stood still and hungry, crouched near a cluster of bushes, terrified of being noticed by one of these hard characters, but desperate for a scrap of something to eat. Barley could tell that these people were broken, and he could also tell that they knew it. Barley could sense their desolation just by watching them from a distance through the hazy mist that swarmed over the eerie scene.

At the fire closest to him was a small group, just three people.

The first man was short and stocky, with a hard, squat body, a mop of ragged light brown curls on his head, and a thin, patchy beard dotting a red face that shone with sweat. He was sitting on top of a large rock near the fire and noisily slurping wine from a broken piece of pottery. He had a loud, rude voice, and the other two called him "Hog," which was an appropriate nickname.

Near him was a woman with long reddish hair, who looked to Barley like she had once been very pretty. She was lying against a man who sat by the fire, using his thigh as a pillow for her snoring head.

This man was a taller fellow, Barley could see by his

long legs, which were stretched out on the ground. He was cooking something on a long stick that he held idly over the flames. He had dark brown hair and a beard. His body was thin, but he had sinewy muscles that made him look strong. His nose looked like it had been flattened by boyhood fights, but in a way that made some men's faces look more interesting, or manly, or wise to the ways of life.

"Arrrgggh! Give me! Give me! You . . . you . . . aaarrrgh!"

Barley heard the very loud and very disturbing sound.

In a flash, a very old man hurled himself like a speeding ghost from a bush near where Barley was standing. As fear streaked through Barley's body, the old man fell hard onto the ground a few feet from Barley, screaming.

"Aaahhhhh! Nooo! Mine!"

He was followed, a second later, by a younger man who was grabbing him and trying to take something from the old man's hand.

Barley instinctively backed away. As he did, the two men fought in a way that made their bodies and squealing voices seem like a single, ridiculous animal. As their violent and awkward wrestling continued, the stocky fellow Barley had noticed sitting by the fire, the one known as Hog, began to laugh loudly at the sight.

The strong-looking man with the interesting nose stood straight up. He took a few quick, robust strides over to where the two men were scuffling. As he approached, Barley could see by the confident glare in this tall man's eyes that he was going to take charge of things. And sure enough, the man grabbed the attacker's collar and with one nimble but forceful motion, wrenched the stunned man off the old fellow and launched the bully into the air—so fast and so far that the would-be attacker toppled back onto his humiliated backside.

Barley was impressed. He stood in the shadows, watching as the old man's protector finished dispatching the young rogue.

"Make trouble again and I'll shove you into the fire," the strong man said through gritted teeth. Then he pointed at the still-laughing Hog and said, "And I'll let that fat man over there eat your sneaky little carcass for supper!"

The young man stood up nervously and, after taking one look at the fight-hardened body and ferocious expression of the man who'd just flattened him, ran away as fast and as far as he could.

Once the troublemaker was gone, the strong man turned to the ghostly-eyed fellow, who was clutching whatever the other man had tried to get from his tightly clenched hands.

"You are not hurt, old man. Don't fear. He won't trouble you again."

The old man mumbled words that no one could understand, pulled what he was protecting in his hands tightly to his chest, and finally said one tentative word.

"B-b-bread."

"No fears, old sir. I won't let anyone take your bread. It's good that you know to hold it tight."

And the old man said it again.

"Bread . . ."

Then he showed the man who had saved him what he was clutching so tightly and trying to protect.

It was a stone.

CHAPTER 6

S amid.

That's what the strong man was called.

Barley watched as Samid picked up the stick he was using to roast a very sorry-looking chunk of meat. Samid gave it a sniff and returned it to the fire to finish cooking. As the fatty meat roasted, the smell was carried on the wind to Barley's snout. But since a dog's instinct is to focus on potential danger first and food next, Barley was focused first and foremost on observing this group of humans to see if they were dangerous or approachable.

"Hey, Samid." The stout guy laughed at the taller in a way that told Barley this was the name of the man he liked. "Why did you bother that guy?"

"He stole," Samid said bluntly.

"So. I stole that," Hog chuckled, pointing to the sizzling meat his friend was roasting. "I stole it from Cracked Amos—I told you."

"I don't like Cracked Amos," Samid said. "I like that old guy."

"Then why didn't you beat the guy who stole half to death, like you usually do?" Hog laughed his nasty laugh. "I could use the entertainment."

"Because there's a lady present," Samid said.

"Prisca is no lady," Hog sniggered as he nudged the woman. "This tarty baggage?"

"Shut your rude face." Samid was serious.

"Samid's gone soft," Hog sneered.

"You'll see how soft I am when I break your face for you!"

"You can't hit me," Hog jeered. "There's a lady present."

"But the lady can hit you," Prisca said as she gave Hog the back of her hand, knocking him off the rock so that his wine splattered all over the ground. Samid and Prisca roared with laughter, and Hog screamed a stream of words that included "wench," "hellcat," "fool," "plague," and "dung."

Barley had seen and heard enough to know these

were very different creatures from Adah and Duv. Their voices were not soft and kind. These people spoke harshly, laughed gruffly, and touched each other in a way that Barley didn't know was playing or fighting. This scared Barley—but there was also something intriguing about their ways.

"This meat smells rancid," Hog grumbled.

"We're fortunate to have it," Prisca said.

"The fortunate don't live in this pit," Samid said, taking the stick out of the dying fire. He laid the meat on a large rock and began to divide it up, tearing pieces off as its musky juices dripped over the small, severed chunks.

Barley stood there smelling the meat. The hunger he had been ignoring suddenly felt bottomless. But as starved as he was, Barley was still too scared to move near the food or the fire. Though he imagined how nice it would be to take a big bite out of the juicy meat, he had already seen what had happened to the fellow who tried to steal from the old man.

Instead, Barley lay on his belly, his paws in front of him, staring longingly at the food. He resolved to remain still, sitting there, watching quietly.

What Barley did not know was that the distressing events of the day—the panic, the sadness, the running, the hunger, the cold, the loneliness, the memories of his mother, the loss of Adah and Duv—were rising up inside him and, without realizing it, he was too exhausted to hold it all back.

Without even meaning to, Barley had begun to cry.

The soft whimpers came out of Barley involuntarily, high-pitched and plaintive. And then a loud sound escaped from his salivating mouth and, in one full note, rang through the air.

Barley had accidentally barked at the meat.

The heads of the three people at the fire turned with a quick twist toward the sound, and Barley saw three sets of surprised eyes staring at him. His thin legs quivered with fear.

And then something wonderful happened.

The lips of the strong man named Samid parted, and Barley noticed two things. First, some of the man's teeth were broken. But the second thing Barley noticed was that he didn't care what sort of teeth the man had, because the fact was, this man—who had been surprised by the presence of Barley—was now smiling.

"Well, well, well," Samid said cheerily, his flattened nose widening out into a fully grinning face. "What have we here?"

"It's a dog," offered Hog.

"Thank you, idiot. I know that."

Then Prisca spoke up. "Samid, he could be dangerous—wild or vicious."

But Samid said with a grin as he peered over at Barley, "That little thing? No."

Then the squat man piped in with, "Throw a rock at it, Samid!"

"Shut your nasty mouth! No one's throwing anything at him. I think it's a him."

Prisca laughed and said, "Looks hungry. And most hims usually do."

Samid took the stick with the roasting meat out of the fire. He tore off a juicy hunk and lifted it toward his mouth.

Barley thought it was hard enough to watch him roast it, but watching this man eat it would be unbearable.

But instead of putting it in his mouth, Samid blew on it a few times.

Then he did something that amazed Barley. He reached out his hand that was holding the meat right in the direction of Barley. He gazed into Barley's eyes, smiling with his broken teeth, and said enticingly, "Come here . . . boy."

Barley was hungrier than he had ever been in his life, and the meat he was gazing at dripped warm and luscious. Barley was also pleased because the man had called him "boy." Even though his name was Barley, on his evening walks with Duv—the evening walk Barley never got to go on tonight—Duv would call him "Barley boy."

Barley began to walk tentatively toward the meat, inching forward slowly as Samid reassured him.

"Here, boy . . . Here you go . . . Come here . . . This is for you."

Barley finally got close enough for Samid to hold the meat right in front of his face. Barley opened his mouth slightly, closed his teeth down around the soft meat, took it slowly from the man's hand, and, lying down on his belly and using his paws to hold and maneuver it, had his first food in many hours. As Barley gnawed, the man petted the top of Barley's head with a hand that felt almost as rough as tree bark, but that moved with gentleness up and down Barley's small head.

Hog poured some wine from his jug into the palm of his hand and held it out toward Barley, laughing.

"Here, dog. Wash it down with some wine—"

Moving so fast and roughly it scared Barley, Samid swatted Hog's hand away, splashing the wine into the fire, and grabbed the stocky little man by the throat.

"Don't you dare give wine to my dog, you fool!"

"Your dog?"

And then Samid smiled as Barley went back to eating, and he went back to petting, and Hog sipped what wine was left in his clay cup.

Though happily occupied eating, Barley did wonder at how this man could go so quickly from kind to angry and then back to nice again.

But he liked this man.

"Watch him. I'll be right back."

And Samid got up and walked away. Barley hoped the man would come back, because the two people he was left with seemed meaner. The lady less so, but the squat man who tried to give Barley the wine was someone Adah would have called a "no-good one."

"Samid," Hog yelled laughingly into the dark, "find some more wine, or I'm going to roast your dog!"

From far off, Barley heard Samid yell back, "I'll roast you with an apple in your mouth, like the pig you are!"

Hog went back to sipping the last of his wine as the lady came over and began to pet Barley in a way that made him like her a little more. Unlike Samid, her teeth were intact and pretty. She had green eyes and dark eyebrows and a voice that was a bit husky and sad-sounding. Barley liked the way she softly tickled him under his chin with one hand and reached down and scratched the front of his belly with her long nails.

After a few moments of this, he rolled over onto his back, content to be comforted. He was only there for a few moments when he flipped over and back up onto his legs, because the man he liked had returned. Barley looked up into the strong face and the dark brown of his red-rimmed eyes.

Then, before he ever saw it coming, a *rope*!

It flew by Barley's snout and down around his neck, encircling his throat with a loop made from a knot tied by Samid.

Barley's whole body cramped with terror, and chattering shakes of panic instantly overtook his small body.

Samid laughed.

"What? Afraid of a little rope?"

And he laughed again.

"No, boy—it's good. It won't hurt you. See?"

Samid petted Barley with a few reassuring strokes, then gently pushed up the slipknot he'd made in the rope till it was close to Barley's neck but not around it too tight.

"See, boy? This won't hurt. It'll just keep you with me. This place can be dangerous."

And he reassured his now-leashed dog with calm laughs and affectionate strokes until Barley's shakes lessened. And soon he was no longer scared at all. Barley had eaten. He was near a fire. A lady was petting him, and a kind and brave man was calling him "boy." For the first time in many hours, Barley wagged his tail—lazily, contentedly, at peace.

Hog saw that Prisca was holding a piece of the meat and snarled, "If you're not eating that, give it here."

"I'm saving it," she said, and wrapped it gently in a piece of rag.

"It won't taste any better later."

"I'm going to bring it to Boaz the flute player."

"Why?" Hog protested gruffly. "He plays in the city for coins and never shares with us beggars."

Samid kicked Hog's leg hard, making him bray a loud "Ouch!"

"Don't call me a beggar," Samid said, his eyes aimed threateningly. Hog could tell Samid was serious, so he lowered his head contritely.

"Call me a thug, call me dirt, but if you call me a beggar again, I'll kill you." Then Samid turned to Prisca. "Prisca, Hog's right. Why bring food to Boaz who never shares with anyone?"

"He shares music. And he plays beautifully."

Samid stared at her.

"All right," she said after a silence. "Because I have begun to believe that we should treat others as we want to have people treat us. That's what the Teacher says."

For a moment, no one talked, as Barley's eyes darted between all three of them, wondering what they were discussing and sensing it was important.

Then Prisca crouched on the ground till she was face-to-face with Barley. She looked into Barley's eyes, the way people sometimes do. She whispered half to herself, half to Barley, "Do to others as you would have them do to you."

Then she tousled Barley's scruffy head.

"You understand, I bet—even if they don't. Don't you, boy?"

Barley liked the soft look in Prisca's eyes and the gentle tone of her voice, so he wagged his tail.

Samid looked down at her petting his dog, a glow from the fire falling across her pretty face, the little dog returning her soft gaze. Then Prisca stood up and, without another word, began walking toward Boaz's hovel while Samid and Hog watched her.

Samid was quiet. But Hog, of course, spoke right up.

"She's been like this lately, repeating what she's heard from that teacher from Galilee everyone in the city's been talking about. I think he's dangerous. What do you think?" he asked Samid, who was still staring after Prisca as she disappeared into the darkness.

"I think you should mind your own matters."

After walking alongside Samid for about a hundred paces, Barley came to a small tent pitched beneath the shade of a thin tree, where at the moment a piece of Samid's underclothes hung drying. This was a place that could never be called a home. The small hovel-like tent consisted of various strips of cloth and pieces of old lambskin, all tied together with odd bits of knotted rope. Two sticks, about five feet apart from each other, held one side of this ragged enclosure, and the other side was fixed to the ground with rocks and stick-spikes that kept the structure from being blown to tatters by the desert wind. Under this narrow shelter there was only enough room for Samid and his meager possessions, which included a few pieces of frayed clothing, two jugs, a large stick he used for protection, and a few other shoddy items.

When they arrived at this small shelter, Samid tied the rope onto the small tree next to it and crawled into his tent.

Barley tried to follow him, but the rope wouldn't reach. When Samid saw him trying to get into the tent, he gave Barley a shove and shouted angrily, "No! Stay out!"

Barley crouched and lowered his head contritely.

Barley had seen this same flash of sudden anger earlier when Samid had attacked Hog. Barley's instincts told him that he should continue to be wary, tread lightly, and stay alert. This man was not Duv. And this camp, crawling with rough-edged souls, was not Adah's warm hearth.

Barley lay out flat, his belly on the ground. The night air was cold, and the pebble-strewn ground felt rough on Barley's belly. But he didn't dare move. He just looked up at Samid with an exhausted and mournful glance.

Samid stretched out on the ground. He reached for his

heavy cloak and drew it up over his thin, hardened body. Then Samid put an old sack filled with leaves under his head and turned away.

Barley curled himself up into a ball, trying to stay warm.

Though life was very different at the end of this long day than it had been when the day began, Barley was grateful for what he had. He had food and a new master. He was cold, but he was alive.

As Barley lay beside Samid's tent waiting for sleep to come, he thought about his mother and her care for him during those first blurry weeks of his life. He thought about Adah and Duv and the years of warm nights by their fireside, the walks and the games of fetch, Adah's kitchen with its lovely aromas, and Duv's impish-eyed birds.

Barley tried to push his body down into the dirt and pretend that the cold earth was the curve of his mother's belly or the warm floor of Adah and Duv's kitchen. He hoped he would fall asleep quickly and have good dreams. He breathed a few comforting, slow breaths and began to nod off.

Then Barley heard movement close by.

It was Samid. He had emerged from his tent and untied the rope from the tree.

Barley looked up at him.

"Well . . . come in."

Barley hesitated.

"It's all right, boy. Come on."

Barley got up slowly and walked tentatively into the tent. Once inside, Samid got back under his cloak and laid his head down on the pillow with his face toward Barley.

After a few seconds, Barley went over to a small pile of clothes on the floor. He gave the clothes a quick sniff and then walked right into the middle of the heap. Samid watched as Barley turned around three times, walked in a tight circle, and finally plopped his little body down in the middle of the clothes with a comfortable thud. Samid could see Barley's ears and a bit of his tiny black nose sticking up from his small mound of ragged clothes. Samid grinned his broken-toothed grin, and the two of them fell asleep.

CHAPTER 7

It was almost completely good. That was how the next day unfolded for Barley. Almost completely happy. The sun had come up, the sky was cloudless, and a mildly cool wind blew away some of the smoke and stench that had hung over the camp all night. In such cheerful weather, even the crooked-looking characters of this place, who were so scary at nighttime, appeared to Barley in the daylight to be only interesting, as opposed to frightening.

Maybe this place could become a home that he would eventually come to enjoy.

Throughout the day, he followed Samid around the

camp and met many new people. Some people's faces brightened as soon as they saw Barley coming their way, led proudly by Samid. Those people would smile broadly, showing teeth worse even than Samid's. Some of them seemed a little frightened of Barley—a reaction he had never gotten from people before. But most of the people who were scared of him looked to Barley like they might be afraid of everything. Like the one man sitting crouched under a threadbare blanket, peering out vacantly and clutching a carved wooden flute in his gnarled hands.

"Hi, Boaz," Samid yelled as he and Barley walked past. "Are you feeling better?"

Boaz nodded his head yes and said in a quivering voice, "Prisca gave me food . . . m-m-meat."

"I know. It was nice of her."

Then Samid called out to the man, "Will you play for us?" Samid made the motions of playing an imaginary flute as he whistled a tune. But Boaz just stared at him glassy-eyed and then turned away.

Samid had noticed Barley's reaction to his whistling. Barley tilted his head in a way that made Samid laugh.

"If you like that, boy, wait till you hear this!"

He left Barley sitting alertly right where he was and moved several paces away. Then he turned and looked right at Barley. Samid drew his upper lip down, put the tip of his tongue between his teeth, and blew a sound so loud and clear and bright that Barley grew wings and flew to his master, who crouched down to catch him and shower him with a celebration of pats and praise.

Samid tried it once more—same whistle, same result. Then he walked along, high-stomached with pride. It was probably the first time he'd taught anyone anything. To Barley, his master's whistle was like the funny voice used by the boy who played in the fields of Barley's memory, or like his name being spoken lovingly again and again during his seven happy years with Adah and Duv. Samid's whistle was the new signal-song of the man to whom Barley now knew he belonged.

Dusk came softly to the camp, and the temperature didn't drop nearly as much as it had the night before.

So all in all, his first day at the camp had proven to be a good day for Barley.

Except for one problem.

No food.

And after so many new sights and sounds and activities, Barley was ready for a bowl of Adah's fine supper. But here, in this new home, there was no Adah and no supper.

Not only did Samid not have any food, but there didn't seem to be any around in the entire camp, except for the one piece of bread that Prisca had, which was so old and hard it had to be divided between her, Samid, and Hog using a large piece of thin rock. And even this stale bread hadn't turned up until very late in the day, when it was already dark.

Barley had watched the three of them eating and feared he would not get any bread. But Samid did what good masters do and fed his dog a piece of his own ration. While the challenging chew of this bread felt good on Barley's teeth, it didn't do much to fill his belly. That night Barley went to sleep hungry.

Early the next morning, Barley looked up and saw the first streaks of morning light, then rolled over to nod back off, certain that—just like the day before—Samid and the other denizens of this place would sleep the morning away. But when Barley looked Samid's way, Samid was still lying down but looking up thoughtfully, staring at the threadbare roof of his tent like something was on his mind.

Since his master wasn't stirring, Barley curled himself back into a tight ball, pushed his head even deeper into the comfortable pile of Samid's clothes, and was just drowsing back off to sleep when he heard the sound of someone approaching Samid's tent—and the loud voice of Hog.

"Samid! Samid! Get up!"

"Hog? What do you want?"

Hog appeared, suddenly landing on his melon-size

knees at the entrance to Samid's small tent and sticking his head in rudely. He was clearly upset about something.

"I've had enough. I've got to get some food."

"We all feel the same way. So don't come barging in to talk about it! It just makes me even hungrier, you pest!"

While this banter was very different from the early morning pleasantries Barley was accustomed to hearing Adah and Duv exchange, he lay there, morning-lazy and content, listening to the two men.

"Are you telling me, Samid, that you've been able to think of anything else but bread? Or meat? Or maybe even meat with herbs and sweet milk . . ."

"Shut up, Hog! And get out of here," shouted Samid.

Hog looked over at Samid. "I'm thinking of going into town. Come with me. There's nothing to be had in this hell-hole, and we have to do something to get some food."

"I don't beg, Hog. You're free to go to town and stand there with your palm up hoping citizens will toss you a crumb as they walk by holding their noses. I'd rather starve."

Barley raised himself up and ambled over to Samid. He lay down on the ground alongside his master, his eyes closing in half-sleep as Samid rested his huge, square-knuckled hand on Barley's small head.

Hog leaned forward to Samid and said in an exaggerated whisper, "I'm not talking about begging."

At this Samid lifted his head and glanced knowingly at Hog.

"No, Hog. These days are not a time to be picking pockets. People who come back here from being in the city say the marketplace is overrun with Roman soldiers itching to punish rabble like us."

Hog became more emphatic. "I'm not talking about the marketplace and I'm not talking about picking pockets. That takes too much patience, and my belly is out of patience," he said in a tone that was hushed but overenunciated. Samid began to listen.

"I've heard about a place some merchants are using as a shortcut. A breach in the city wall, near the Shepherd's Crook. The unlicensed merchants use it to sneak their goods into town without having to get past the Roman soldiers at the gate."

There was silence as Hog waited for Samid's reaction.

"No," Samid said after a prolonged pause, trying hard to inject firmness into his voice.

"Aren't you hungry?"

He was.

Although having a dog around was a good distraction—and distraction is the only hope for a mind in the grip of a body's hunger.

Hog pressed, "All we've eaten in two and a half days is a finger's worth of badger gristle!"

Samid's mind turned to thoughts of their meal two days before and the look on Prisca's face in the firelight as she wistfully spoke those strange words. *"Do to others . . ."*

He was snapped back to the present by Hog's insistent whining.

"I'm weak," moaned Hog, loud enough that Barley cocked an eye.

"Today is Sunday, right? Town will be full of people, no?"

"Yes. And last night Prisca said she heard town will be even busier than usual because there are rumors that crackbrained, so-called holy man from Galilee is coming today. Prisca left at dawn to try to see him," Hog said nastily. Then he laughed. "Though if he is so holy, what would he want with the likes of her!"

"Hold your dirty tongue," mumbled Samid, lost in thought.

"Oh, never mind about that one. Didn't you hear me? There'll be even more people in town than usual. And that means—"

"I know," Samid interrupted. "It means such demand that even the worst of the bakers and butchers will be lugging their wares to town."

"And willing on a Sunday to be—maybe—charitable."

Samid rolled over and stared at Barley.

"We have to go now, Samid," said Hog.

"All right," said Samid, both intently and with defeat in his voice.

"To the Shepherd's Crook."

The journey into the city was an enjoyable one for Barley. Samid and Hog walked at a rapid clip, with Barley trotting close on Samid's heels, his little legs working quickly to keep up with Samid's large, worn sandals. Every few minutes, Hog would become exhausted from lugging his huge frame around and would crouch with his hands resting on his knees, panting loudly from exertion.

"It's not my fault!" Hog would yell above the chorus of Samid's laughter. "I have short legs!"

In this way, Samid, Hog, and Barley made their way to the place called the Shepherd's Crook.

All three of them stopped a moment to take in the sight as Jerusalem came into view, looming grand and imposing over the desolate desert landscape. As soon as they saw it, Hog collapsed dramatically onto the road and lay there howling, "I am so tired and hungry! I am going to die right here!"

"I'll alert the vultures," said Samid with a roll of his eyes.

Samid could see, off in the distance, the main road that was the official entrance into the city. A group of soldiers stood together—a large, brawny, clanging cluster of red capes, heavy armor, and mountainous shoulders supporting heads with flashing eyes that said nothing would make them happier than to find a citizen or two to harass.

All citizens passing through this gate had to pass the scrutinizing glare of these men unless they knew about the clandestine breach in the wall. The Shepherd's Crook was used of late by itinerant travelers, small-time young ruffians, and lower-class merchants and tradesmen with no official license to sell their goods in public.

The Shepherd's Crook was a long path—too narrow to be called a road—that rested a foot or so lower than the surrounding terrain. It had been formed by one of the city's aqueducts many generations ago. At the end of the path was the entrance to a curving loop of ancient wall—the "crook." Samid had at first wondered if it had been a good idea for him to bring his dog without a rope. But throughout their journey to the city, anytime Samid had whistled, Barley had rushed immediately to his master's side. Even Hog had been impressed, though he was still unhappy that Samid had brought Barley along. Samid picked up a stick and hurled it down the long path, and, to get his mind off his hunger, even Hog tossed it a few times—surprisingly far, Barley noticed, for someone who wheezed when he ran.

The secluded curve of the crook was welcome relief

from the dusty path, and the coolness of the cracked walls and stone floor felt soothing after their long trek. Hog plopped his sweaty body down and leaned his head against the wall.

Samid joined him, stretching out his long legs as Barley stood at his master's side. A stream of water leaking from a fissure in the wall had pooled into a large rut in the rock floor, making what looked to Barley to be a perfect water bowl. He leaned down and began lapping the cool water into his dry mouth with relish as Samid watched, smiling and patting Barley as he drank.

Hog saw Samid grinning down at Barley and said scornfully, "What are you so jolly about?"

"I don't know," Samid said, still looking down at the dog madly slurping up his drink of water. "How small his tongue looks. The sound of it. It's funny. It's . . ."

Samid stopped himself. He blushed at having given Hog a glimpse of his affection for Barley. Barley, meanwhile, basked in the new sweetness that had crept into his master's tone and was happy to feel Samid's strong hand patting his back as he drank.

Hog said with disgust, "I've always hated the way water feels on an empty stomach. I swear, Samid, at this point I'd kill for food if I had to."

Samid squinted into the sun and smiled.

"Hog," he said whimsically, "maybe we shouldn't get into trouble today. Maybe we should just try to have a happy Sunday."

"What?" Hog snapped. "That dumb dog has made you soft." And he turned impatiently and walked toward the entrance of the crook from where they'd come.

"People should have a happy Sunday," Samid continued, turning to Barley. "Right, boy?"

Barley wagged his tail as he drank his last few gulps of water.

"Hello, sir!"

Samid's gaze darted quickly to Hog, who was speaking to someone nearing the entrance of the crook. Barley's eyes focused on his master, and he watched closely as his master's demeanor shifted. Barley saw the sweetness in his master's eyes transform into a hard, alert stare.

Samid leapt to his feet, and Barley followed his master's gaze toward the entrance of the crook. As Barley's snout filled with a mouthwatering scent, a small, gray-haired baker entered the crook carrying a large sack swollen to the brim with round, aromatic loaves of bread.

Hog spoke to the baker fawningly.

"You must be a very skilled baker to make something that smells as good as that nice bread does."

"Yep," the baker said halfheartedly as he trudged ahead,

passing Samid with an idle nod as he headed toward the passage that led to the breach in the city wall.

"My dear man," Hog called out, following the baker, "perhaps you would allow me to help you up those steep stairs with that large sack."

As Hog passed Samid to catch up to the baker, he gave Samid a knowing wink. Barley noticed Samid's muscles tighten and his glare intensify.

"Dear sir," Hog kowtowed as the baker kept walking, "couldn't you use some help from a younger man?" As he walked alongside the man, he pleaded, "You see, sir, I would so like to be able to do a good deed for the Sabbath."

At mention of the Sabbath, the baker slowed his pace long enough to size up Hog, then replied gruffly, "I don't need help. Never have."

Immediately, Samid jumped in, affecting a falsely merry tone. "Oh, don't insult the gentleman, Hog. He doesn't need your help. This is a man who does things his way. And though no youngster, this is a man who carries his own wares."

"Always have," the man agreed, nodding at Samid.

Fortified by Samid's compliment, the baker adjusted his sack of bread proudly and continued on his way, as Hog shot Samid a glance that said, *"Now what?"*

"But," Samid called out, "I bet a clever merchant like

him knows all the best shortcuts in the city. Maybe he can give us directions to Shiloah."

"Yes . . . Shiloah," Hog sang out, understanding what Samid wanted him to do.

"Oh, I know a good way to Shiloah," the baker obliged as he stopped walking.

"My friend and I are going there, and I told him Shiloah is over in that direction," Hog said, deliberately pointing the wrong way.

"Oh no—that's not right. I'll tell how you go. You take . . ." And the baker launched into an elaborate set of directions, pleased to be able to show off his know-how to two lost travelers. As he did, Hog stood in front of him pretending to listen, all the while darting quick glances over the baker's shoulder. Samid was several paces behind the man and had begun inching toward him. Barley watched as Samid moved slowly, smoothly, intently.

The baker was now sketching onto his palm with his finger the last details of the shortcut he was explaining. As he did, he loosened his grip on the shoulder rope of the sack. Now only a foot from the man's back, Samid reached out his hands, spreading his fingers into a large claw and aiming for the slacken rope just an inch from his grasp.

Then, suddenly, voices!

Samid's head snapped around and looked back toward

the entrance of the crook. He heard the sound of men's laughter coming from down the path—a ways off, but quickly approaching. Barley saw the hardness in Samid's eyes evolve into a look of panic. Samid hurtled toward the entrance to the crook, his heart pounding nervously. He poked his head around the curve and saw two merchants walking in his direction. Both were younger men, one of them tall and broad, and they both carried walking staffs.

Samid hissed a warning to Hog in a husky whisper. But Hog was so busy looming closer and closer to the unsuspecting baker that he paid Samid no mind.

"Hog, don't!" Samid called out.

But it was too late. The baker looked up, and as he did, his face met a stunning blow from Hog's meaty fist. The baker staggered backward a few steps, reeling from the blow.

The baker, who was tougher than he appeared, widened his legs, determined to steady himself. Hog reached out and grabbed the baker's sack. Though still stunned by Hog's sharp blow, the baker clung feistily to his bag of bread. Hog kept one hand on the bread sack and put the other one on the nape of the baker's neck. Then he used all the heft of his squat body to drive the man down, face-first, onto the stone ground—so hard the man's nose broke with a crack so loud that the fur on Barley's back rose up.

Barley began to bark as his master ran toward Hog and the baker.

"Stay!" Samid said firmly to Barley.

Hog had ripped the bread sack from the baker's back and now had his hands on the baker's coin purse and was tugging furiously to free it. Though on the ground, his nose dripping blood, the baker was fiery and not about to let his money go. As a stream of curses flew from his mouth, the man curled himself into a ball, his knees touching his chest, and rolled every which way trying to break Hog's stubborn grip on his purse.

Samid tried to pull Hog off of the baker.

"Merchants with sticks are coming up the path, Hog. We have to go! Now!"

Hog screamed into Samid's face, "But I almost have his purse free! And it's a fat one!"

"No, Hog!" Samid bellowed.

The baker was flailing madly at Hog, and as Samid joined in the fray, the man kicked his bony legs up at Samid. When one of these kicks landed hard in Samid's stomach, his demeanor changed.

"Enough," said Samid darkly. "I will end this. Now."

Samid grabbed the front of the baker's tunic and pushed him to the ground. He dropped his full weight down onto the man, plunging his knee into his chest with such force the baker expelled a loud grunt. Then Samid lifted his arms and folded his knuckles into a hammer-like fist held high over the baker's already broken teeth to summon the force he needed to land a finishing blow.

But as he did, Samid caught sight of Barley, now standing just inches from him, looking up at Samid, frightened by what he was seeing.

Samid's raised fist slackened, and Barley saw his master's ruthlessness melt. Samid looked into Barley's eyes and said gently, "Boy . . ."

At Samid's pause, the baker opened his eyes and, in a last burst of do-or-die force, cocked his leg and kicked it forward, aiming right for Samid's exposed throat, but he missed. Instead, the full force of it pounded into Barley's thin body.

The man's foot pounded so deep into Barley's rib cage that all breath was knocked from his body and his thin frame was sent flying across the width of the crook, his pink belly scraping as he slid along the gravel.

Samid's face went ashen as he saw Barley kicked with such crushing force. He rushed to where his dog had landed against a stone wall and reached for Barley, who was squirming to right himself back onto all fours. In one quick motion, Samid scooped his injured dog, pulled Barley into a secure embrace, and turned to hightail it from the crook toward the city.

"Got it!"

Hog's voice rang out from over Samid's shoulder, followed quickly by the sound of ripping leather and the clattering of a hail of coins as they landed in the street.

"Samid! Money!"

But Samid was gone.

CHAPTER 8

On this particular Sunday in the city of Jerusalem, it seemed as though every single citizen had descended upon the teeming marketplace. The pulsating roar of this concentration of humanity echoed down the narrow, deserted street where Samid and Barley crouched in a doorway.

Barley had gasped to take in air the whole while Samid ran, carrying him through the warren of alleyways leading to a narrow side street that eventually opened out into the marketplace. It was only now, when Samid was sure they were not being chased and could rest unseen on this empty side street, that he put Barley down on the ground to have a look at how badly hurt he was.

The heavily winded Hog shortly rounded the corner of the street and huffed and puffed his way toward Samid and Barley.

"Fool!" Hog shouted, wheezing as his pace slowed. "That's what you are!"

Hog kept repeating the word as he shoved thick hunks of bread into his mouth.

"What's wrong with you? If you'd have helped me, I'd have gotten the whole purse, not just what I could scoop up from the ground!" Hog hectored while shaking a fist containing six large coins in it. He looked down at Samid, who was now kneeling by Barley, and said, "That blasted dog. I'm telling you, Samid, you've gone soft."

"You'll see how soft I am when I choke you to death!"

Barley was hurt. And he was confused. His head was lowered, his body was crouched, and his usually wagging tail was curled under his body. His eyes looked up questioningly at Samid.

Samid did his best to reassure his dog as he ran his big hands gently over Barley's body to feel for what he'd seen in his many street fights—the telltale jutting of a broken bone. Barley had none. But his nostrils were crusted with dirt from where he had lain in the gravel road gasping for air.

"Let me see," Samid said, looking closer. Then he put his thumb in his own mouth and gently cleaned his dog's snout as Barley looked up into his eyes trustingly. "It's all right, boy. You're all right."

"An idiot," Hog carried on as he stuffed the last of the bread into his already full mouth, "which makes me a double idiot for trusting you, you big, tall, ugly rat! I'd rather be on my own than with a louse like you. It would serve you right if I went off without you."

"Good. Go," said Samid.

"I will! I'm going to take my six coins and go find myself some good wine and some women! And you and your runty dog can stay here and rot."

"Fine!"

"And may I say, the bread was delicious!" Hog yelled as he turned to waddle his way up the street.

"I don't care," Samid called out to him proudly.

Hog stopped abruptly, turned around, and walked over to Samid.

"Here," he said, holding out his hand, which contained a single shiny coin.

Samid stared at the coin in Hog's hand. He knew it would buy Prisca and his dog a good meal, so with little hesitation, he swallowed his pride, ignored his conscience, and took the coin.

"But one is all you get," Hog muttered, his eyes resting on Samid's face.

Samid smiled begrudgingly. "I'll see you back at camp?"

"I may be very drunk."

"I think I'll recognize you."

As Hog trudged away, Samid and Barley were left alone on the quiet street.

Samid knelt down on one knee. He reached out gently and took Barley's snout into his hands. Then he bent his face down onto Barley's head and whispered, his lips pressing the words he said right into his dog's fur. "I'm so sorry. Nothing like that will ever happen to you again."

Barley had no idea what Samid was whispering. But it didn't matter. Dogs know that words spoken in this way by a master are always a vow. As Samid looked into his dog's eyes and smiled, he knew that no matter what, this was and always would be his dog. As Barley gazed back at Samid, his head suddenly twitched back and his snout flew forward with a massive sneeze that sent a colossal spray of road dust and dog drizzle into his master's unsuspecting face.

With one eye closed and a wry grin forming, Samid said simply, "Thanks." With that, Barley began wagging his tail, himself once again.

The northern end of Jerusalem was the area where most of the city's inhabitants congregated on Sundays. It was the area of the great temple, a treasure that all citizens—even those who were not religious—were proud of and enjoyed. The northern end of Jerusalem was also a likely destination for visitors to the city. Here was a larger sea of life than anything Barley had experienced before. There were hordes of humans and, every few feet, carts filled with all sorts of unusual items, pulled by horses who stood higher and stronger and wore more colorful trimmings than any Barley had ever seen.

As Samid and Barley moved among the busy scene, Samid kept looking down to be sure Barley was still at his heels, dodging the dangers of the bustling crowd. He was impressed at his dog's agility and knack for keeping up. Samid led Barley to a corner of the plaza that was awash in such good-smelling smoke that Barley tried to take a bite of it as it wafted by him. They had arrived at an area of massive tables where fat-armed butchers lopped and trimmed slabs of meat from spits that hung over fires popping with drippings from the carcasses broiling above. Sometimes a pounding knife would flick a hunk of gristle to the ground, where it was grabbed by the beggars who congregated around these tables. Once, Samid had seen a waif from

Samaria lose his thumb to the cleaver of a cranky butcher as he reached for a scrap of fat, so Samid knew to be canny. As he stood watching a butcher, waiting for his moment to get something—even just a morsel—for him and his dog to eat, there was a sudden commotion behind him.

People began to yell and push and moved in a wave as a massive carriage came into the plaza. The carriage was two-tiered, fancily appointed, and pulled by a pair of enormous horses—one brown, one bright white and red-eyed.

The carriage was driven by a broad man wearing a tunic that was a deep shade of orange Barley had never seen before. It sparkled at the seams and around the edges as elegant bits of adornment caught the sun and glittered, and the effect gave the driver a sheen of self-importance. His beard was long but neatly squared off at the bottom, and though most of the beard was black, a thick streak of pure white ran down the center.

The carriage itself was not the usual rough-hewn, wooden work vehicle Barley was accustomed to. It was almost as colorful as the man's clothes. The body and wheels were painted with curls and flourishes, and the wooden seat the driver sat on was fancily carved and outfitted with a large cushion.

And the cargo of the carriage—that's what really caught Barley's eye.

The carriage was stacked with several long, wide,

wooden cages, each of which was crammed, full-to-bursting, with live birds—all making a loud screeching music that made Barley stare in amazement—and sadness. He had never before seen that many birds, not even in the sky. These caged wretches had none of the bright-eyed personality or natural dignity of the birds Barley had seen Duv make. These birds were crowded and scared and looked out of the cages with hopeless looks in their eyes.

The bird merchant was trying to maneuver his large carriage across the busy plaza, through the dense crowd, and over to the large temple. As the carriage moved near to Barley and Samid, Barley heard a strange sound coming from behind him. At first Barley thought it was another animal, but when he turned around he saw it was an old lady. Her clothes were filthy and ragged, and her chin was hairy with a small gray beard—something Barley had never before seen on a woman. She was smiling and babbling in a singsong way and quite excitedly trying to catch up with the carriage. Once she was next to the carriage, she reached her bent finger into one of the cages and made a kissing sound with her wrinkled lips.

Barley thought she looked very happy.

But then, out of nowhere, the bird merchant's whip came slicing down and lashed her knuckles with a terrible *smack*.

The old woman jumped back in pain, shook her hand

like a small child, and exhaled a high, mournful whimper of unintelligible words.

Samid also was watching and saw what the merchant did to the old woman. He muttered a wrathful string of words under his breath, all of which were new to Barley. But Samid knew this was not a man to challenge in public, and so he turned, making sure Barley was right next to him, and began to walk away as the driver continued hollering.

"Get away from my cart, or I'll run you over, you crazy wench!"

A voice spoke up from within the crowd. "Why would you do that to a poor, hungry old woman?" Then the woman's voice grew louder as she said, "Haven't you heard it said, do to others . . ."

Samid wheeled around, and there stood Prisca. She had positioned herself right in front of the cart.

"How dare you?" The driver scowled down at her as he sat there puffed up with indignation. "A filthy, rag-picking tramp like you should not dare to even speak with someone like me, let alone speak the words of that rebel-rousing Galilean! I have a good mind to give you a . . ."

"You'll give her nothing!"

Samid spoke the words with such volume and authority that every head of every citizen within earshot turned to watch.

"Nothing but an apology!" Samid continued. "Or I'll snap you in half, you petty tyrant."

"Samid!" Prisca gasped. And the crowd gasped along with her, watching tensely, aware that a poor man was now crossing a dangerous line.

Barley could see that whatever his master had just said to the man sent the merchant into a scarlet rage. He knew he could not leave his master's side. The watchful crowd made a pocket of silence in the noisy, busy marketplace as they watched Samid stride over to the man with Barley at his heel. Samid stood below the driver's high seat atop the resplendent carriage, then pushed his face up toward the man and spoke through gritted and broken teeth.

"Listen, you well-fed snake. Watch how you talk to this lady," said Samid, pointing gallantly toward Prisca. "And the next time you mistake a human being for an animal, don't aim your whip at old gray mares—you frilly coward— use it on a horse like me who knows how to kick back."

The man's mouth twisted with rage. He could tell by the look of Samid's ragged garments that he was among the city's castoffs. For a mangy beggar to disrespect a man of his station, and to do so in front of onlookers, was unacceptable, and the merchant needed to save face. He lifted his whip and aimed directly for Samid's back.

But Samid saw it coming.

He caught the whip with his hand and, in spite of the stinging welt it cut into his palm, gripped the whip tightly and yanked it with such force that the merchant was pulled out of his carriage. The flailing man tried to break his fall by grabbing onto a stack of cages, causing several to tip out of the carriage and slam onto the ground, creating a deafening—and comical—cacophony of bird screeching that compelled the crowd to laughter. The merchant landed on the ground on his ample rump, at the center of a hail of falling dove feathers.

Barley barked at the merchant a few times out of support for his master, his barks accompanying the crowd's jeering and snickering.

Prisca saw the burning anger in Samid's eyes as he looked down at the merchant, and she quickly stepped in front of Samid to hold him back, fearing Samid might kill the man.

"Stop, Samid!" she yelled, looking directly into his eyes.

Samid's eyes softened as they stared into Prisca's, and after a brief pause, he let go of the whip, cradled his injured hand in the other, and turned to go.

But when he turned, he found himself staring straight into the enraged face of a Roman soldier in full armor, red cape on his back and an enormous lance in his hand.

The two large men stared at each other, eye to eye, for

several fraught moments, and, for the first time, Barley could actually smell his master's fear.

This made Barley stare at the soldier and growl a low, steady growl that vibrated his thin ribs. As he looked up at his master and the soldier, his little body became very still, his senses heightening, his rhythm slowing.

The soldier, full to brimming with his own authority, bellowed accusingly into Samid's face, "I saw what you did!"

Samid replied heatedly, "But did you see what he did, whipping a poor old lady?" Samid pointed an accusatory finger at the merchant, who by this time was trying to hoist his rotund, orange-adorned frame up off the ground.

"That man," the soldier chided, "is a tax-paying citizen, and you're a piece of wayward scum who walks around stinking up the marketplace. I protect those who deserve protecting."

Samid stared into the soldier's eyes with a strong, steady gaze, and his voice deepened.

"A true man," he said, "and a true soldier, would protect anyone who needs him."

The soldier stood still for a brief moment, stunned into silence by Samid's audacity. Then his face twisted with contempt as he drew his head back, a wad of spit flying from his mouth—like a small, wet whip—onto Samid's face.

Time slowed for Barley as he watched his master react.

A flash of righteous anger flushed Samid's face, and his body coiled with tension as he lifted his hand to wipe the spit from his face. But before the back of Samid's hand could reach his cheek, the soldier, who had gripped his large lance horizontally in his thick, hairy hands, pushed the weapon into Samid's forehead with such a hard blow it snapped Samid's head back on his neck and shocked him momentarily senseless.

Barley began to bark—as loudly and ferociously as a dog three times his size. The soldier had hurt his master, and Barley knew his duty was to help Samid.

Barley stepped closer to the soldier, who—surprising even Barley himself—seemed to be intimidated by his scrappy barks, as though he had an inborn fear of dogs. The soldier instinctively pointed his lance down at Barley, but Barley was undeterred. He dug his paws into the ground—with the full load of his twenty-five pounds of pressure—lowered his head, and sprang at the soldier.

Fortunately, before Barley arrived at his destination, Samid caught Barley in midair and held him tight as he took off running. Samid aimed their escape straight into the crowd, where he knew they could lose the soldier. As Barley lay cradled in his master's arms, he continued to bark in the direction of the soldier—determined to have the last word.

As Samid and Barley fled, Prisca gave them a head start by grabbing onto the soldier's cape and pleading with him.

"Why must you hurt people like us? We already have nothing, not even our pride. You're a cruel, inhuman brute!" The soldier shook his shoulders to loosen Prisca's grip on his cape, and she fell to the ground as he turned away from her with a sneer. And with that, she gathered herself up and ran as fast as she could after Samid and Barley.

Prisca pushed through the crowd, following the sound of Barley's distinct barks till she caught up with Samid. Soon they had made their way far enough into the throng to be sure that the bullying soldier was not chasing them. Samid slowed his pace and lowered himself to let Barley leap out of his arms. Samid and Prisca leaned on each other, panting and shaking their heads with relief that they had executed a successful escape.

After a few moments, Samid finally wiped away the soldier's spittle from his cheek as Prisca looked up at him to see how badly his head was hurt. The soldier's lance had broken the skin, and a nasty purple mark was already swelling into a lump. Prisca touched his forehead gingerly, and Samid winced.

As the two of them looked at each other, Samid shook

his head and asked sadly, his voice thick with emotion, "Why do they hate us so?"

Prisca smiled back gently and said, "They don't hate us. They just don't want to be reminded of us."

"Let's go," Samid said softly.

The three of them walked across the crowded plaza toward a low wall behind which was a cistern filled with runoff water. Samid sat on the wall, glad to be away from the tumult of the crowd, and leaned over to the water to wash the blood from his wound. Prisca sat next to him on one side, and Barley hopped up onto the low wall and sat down on the other.

Samid smiled as he dried his face on the neckline of his tunic, and the tone of his voice suddenly changed from a man defeated to a man who had something nice to give to a lady.

"Prisca," he asked coyly, "when was the last time you ate something?"

"Not too long ago," she fibbed unconvincingly. "I'll . . . I'll beg for something later on."

"No. You won't beg," Samid said happily. "And it won't be later on. Prisca," he sang out jovially, "I am going to buy you the best meal you've ever had."

Samid reached into his tunic, took out the coin Hog had

given him, and held it up in front of Prisca's face. "Look!" he said proudly, watching the gleam of the noonday sun catch the coin's silver shine.

Prisca's eyes gleamed as bright as the coin.

"Oh, Samid . . . !"

Samid put the coin into Prisca's hand, the fingertips of his rough hand grazing the softness of her palm as he placed it there.

"Where did you get it?"

"Never mind where I got it. With that lovely little coin, you and I can, for once, buy a meal. A really good meal."

Prisca looked into his eyes. "Samid . . . did you steal it?"

Samid stared back at her, and his eyes showed a fleeting glint of guilt before they turned up at the corners.

"No," he said with a broad and reassuring smile.

At this Prisca's face lit up as well. "Then this is wonderful!"

"So let's get you some food!" Samid cheered, filled with the mix of relief and shame liars feel when they've been believed.

Just as Samid and Prisca stood and began to walk through the plaza, with Barley close behind them, a man came running past them, heading toward a spot on the far side of the plaza where a crowd was beginning to form.

"The Teacher from Galilee! He's coming!"

The words were whispered, but they issued from the stranger's mouth with intense passion. And Prisca heard them.

"Samid, wait!" she said with such intensity that it startled Samid and made Barley put his ears up.

"Here," she said, trying to put the coin back into Samid's hand. "I can't let you use that to buy me some sort of . . . feast."

"Why not?" Samid asked, refusing to take the coin from her.

"Instead of buying expensive food for me"—her eyes lit up with an idea—"let's use the coin to buy food to bring back to the camp to share with the people there."

"The camp?" said Samid, surprise in his voice. "Why would we use our money to feed the people in the camp?"

"Because they are hungry," answered Prisca. "And because we both know how much hunger hurts everything— our stomachs, our hearts, our dignity, our souls. And the Teacher from Galilee knows this as well. He has said that we should love our neighbors as we love ourselves."

"Well," Samid sneered, "this Teacher has never met our neighbors. He'd change his mind."

"Don't mock, Samid," Prisca said. "I'm serious."

Then she looked away, toward the gathering crowd.

"Samid, the Teacher from Galilee is the reason I came to the city today. To see him with my own eyes."

Then she swallowed hard.

"And maybe . . . to follow him."

"What?" Samid was stricken by her confession and said feebly, "But . . . why?"

"His words," she said simply. "They haunt me. What I've heard has given me a little hope that . . . perhaps . . . I can change the wretched life I've been leading. That may be a lot to ask for someone like me, but people say this Teacher can do miracles."

Samid could not believe his ears. Hearing something like this come from the mouth of the usually sensible Prisca shocked him.

"I don't believe in miracles," he said.

"But I do, Samid. And I am weary of the ugliness of our lives and want mine to change. I believe it can."

"Life doesn't change much for people like us, Prisca."

"Oh, Samid," said Prisca, near tears, "that is so hopeless."

Insulted by her reaction, Samid said dismissively, "Well, that's what I believe."

"So," she said, smiling knowingly, "you believe in despair, but not in the miracle that could save you from it."

Samid had no response.

"Do you think I am a fool to want to change?"

"No," he said bluntly, "but I think you're a fool to believe that someone like me can change."

"Samid, I think that in your heart, you are a good man."

"You're wrong."

"I have faith that you are."

"Then your faith is wrong. I'm not a good man, Prisca."

Then he took a deep breath and turned away. When he finally began to speak again, his tone was softer than usual, and sadder.

"I've done bad things in life, been mean and drunk and stole . . ."

Samid stopped abruptly to swallow back the wave of feeling that, to his surprise, had found its way into his voice.

Barley stared up at Samid. It was his first realization that his master was not always strong.

"I'm not a good man, Prisca," Samid said gently. "I've wanted to be good, and sometimes even tried. But always gotten it wrong."

Prisca reached up and took Samid's face in her hands.

"Just a few moments ago," she said confidently, "I watched the man that I am looking at right now stand up to a brute who was hurting a broken old lady."

She smiled. Samid lowered his eyes.

"And just a few moments before that," he said, "the man you're looking at right now took a coin from a baker he left bleeding in the street."

Prisca was silent for a moment.

"Oh . . ." she said sadly. And then she withdrew her hands from his face, took Samid's hands in hers, and pressed the coin into his palm.

Samid lowered his eyes.

"Go, Prisca. Go find your Teacher."

Prisca touched his shoulder gently, then turned to walk away. As she did, Barley's wagging tail gradually wound down to near stillness.

Prisca suddenly turned back toward Samid and Barley.

"Don't you know what a miracle is, Samid?" And with her pretty smile, quivering now with a touch of sadness, she said, "It's the opposite of despair."

And with that, Prisca disappeared into the swelling crowd.

CHAPTER 9

W ine," muttered Samid. "I must find wine. Where is Hog when I need him?"

Samid looked around as if in a daze, then looked down at Barley. Barley's eyes had followed Prisca until she disappeared into the crowd, and now he looked up at his master quizzically, his head cocked to one side as though he simply couldn't fathom why Samid wasn't following her.

Samid's gaze wandered toward the far end of the plaza known as the stables, a place where lowly workers and merry drunks hung about amid a stink of animals and rubbish so rank that even the soldiers stayed away. He started to walk in that direction, but the crowd in the plaza had suddenly swelled to such density that his view was quickly obscured. The emotion of the citizens seemed so heightened that Samid knew something unusual was taking place. And he and his small dog were now in the middle of it. Samid reached down and hoisted Barley up, resting his dog's belly on one of his strong forearms.

It was a perch Barley found to be both a comfy seat and a fine vantage point from which to take in the excitement of the swarm of people around him. A rather odd-looking fellow stood next to Samid and Barley. He had long, thin cheeks, an even longer and thinner nose, and jutting front teeth that made his whole face look like it was in a perpetual half smile. When the man noticed Barley, the half smile became a full smile. He kept looking down at Barley and then back up at Samid in the way that some strangers do when they want to initiate a conversation.

But Samid was the wrong target for a friendly chat, especially right now. Upon noticing the man's obvious interest in Barley, Samid returned his solicitous smiles with a scowl. But the man was not deterred in the least by Samid's disinterest. Glancing down at Barley again and then back up to Samid, he said with a toothy grin, "Is this your dog?"

"No, it's my camel," Samid muttered.

The intrepid man put his face close to Samid's, looked

at his forehead, and said, "You have a wound. Were you in a fight?"

Samid replied curtly, "That's none of your concern, now, is it?"

The man merely smiled amiably and said, "The Teacher from Galilee has told us, 'If anyone slaps you on the right cheek, turn to them the other cheek also.'"

"Well, that doesn't sound like very wise advice," Samid replied, and walked deeper into the crowd.

The mass of people was now surging forward toward the thoroughfare connecting the plaza to the city's main entry gate. Some people were pushing merely to get a good view of whatever was about to happen, but others looked as though they knew what they were going to see and moved toward the road with a sense of intense expectation.

Barley's senses were highly alert as he gazed at the scene in front of him.

The crowd pushed from behind until Samid and Barley were now near the edge of the thoroughfare. The eyes of the thronging citizens lining the road were all pointed intently at the city gate, and Barley felt swept up in the anticipation. There was a gust of noise up near the gate, and Barley got so excited that he began to pedal his little legs in the air from his perch atop his master's arm, his nails scratching Samid's waist. Samid—with half a laugh and half an ouch—said, "Calm down, boy! We don't know yet what we're about to see!"

Barley looked up the street excitedly as a huge cry erupted from the crowd. As the sea of people parted respectfully to let the procession through, Barley finally saw what was heading his way.

He did, indeed, think it was a remarkable sight—but only because of how unremarkable it was, considering the crowd's ardent anticipation.

Barley saw no ornate carriage, no colorful garments, no majestic horses, nothing at all grand or fancy in any way. All Barley saw was a very kind-looking man riding a small donkey.

It was a sight so simple that Barley could have seen it any day of the week in the neighborhood where he lived with Adah and Duv. However, the people who had gathered around this man on the donkey seemed awestruck by him. They were looking at him with the sort of love that people might have for a king or a hero. Many people were carrying huge, bright green palm leaves, and some were waving the leaves in a way that made it look to Barley like the whole crowd was moving as one. As the man on the donkey rode down the street, many of the citizens ran into the middle of the road and laid the leafy fronds on the stone road for the donkey to walk on.

As soon as Barley could see the man's face, he felt the same way about him. This was someone to honor.

He didn't know exactly why, except that an instinct—a new one, which felt to him like it came from somewhere very deep inside him—told him so.

The Kind Man's eyes were very gentle, and they looked around at the crowd as if he knew everyone in it—even their secrets. And when his eyes moved toward the part of the crowd where Barley was, Barley felt as though a warm wind were blowing right into his chest—a feeling he'd had only one other time in his life, when his mother looked at him on the last day he ever saw her.

The Kind Man's dark brown hair was long, but his beard and eyebrows were neat. His nose was strong and thin, and his lips were soft and content. He wore a thin cloak made of unremarkable material that was off-white—similar to the color of Barley's fur. But the garment was so clean it seemed to glow in the afternoon sunlight. The Kind Man seemed a bit taller and perhaps a tad thinner than the average man, and it looked as though the donkey was having no trouble whatsoever bearing the Kind Man's weight.

The donkey was a brownish gray and young enough that the hair on his haunches still looked soft. He had a white splotch right between his funny eyes and flaring nose, and he looked to Barley like he was a little scared or perhaps worried he wasn't doing a good job. But Barley could also tell that the donkey felt tremendous pride. The donkey held his head high, and even with his awkward gait, Barley thought he looked—and must have felt—like a beautiful, important horse.

It was a small, almost imperceptible gesture that did the most to show Barley the depth of the Kind Man's kindness. It was the way he touched the donkey. Every so often, the Kind Man would gently pat the beast's sweaty haunches in a reassuring way. And once in a while, he would touch the spiky, patchy hair that ran down the beast's back. The Kind Man touched the mane with his long fingers, tousling the tufts gently, twirling some with his index finger, letting the donkey know he loved him and thought he was doing a very good job.

As the Kind Man and his donkey progressed down the thoroughfare, the street began to fill up with so many palm leaves that the stones of the street became invisible beneath the festive green carpet. Citizen after citizen came forward to lay down their tributes to the Kind Man, many of them whispering in reverent tones as they did.

Barley was transfixed by the warmth of the Kind Man, the pride of the donkey, and the joy of the people that seemed to fill the air with a powerful sense of hope.

By now the donkey and the Kind Man were within feet

of Samid and Barley. Barley craned his head back to look up into his master's face. As Samid stared at the approaching Teacher, his face flushed with enough feeling that Barley could sense by what he saw in his master's face that he'd been right to sense the Kind Man was important.

How fine a master must this Kind Man be, to be looked at in awe by masters?

Samid was silent and still as the Teacher and his donkey passed in front of him. Barley looked up toward the Kind Man. No moving, no wagging, just looking up. And somehow Barley could feel that *that* was enough, that it wasn't what Barley *did* that mattered to the Kind Man; what mattered was that Barley was there. And for a few long moments, it felt to Barley as though time had stopped. In a good way.

Barley was snapped out of his reverie when his master suddenly let out a quick gasp. Barley looked up to see that his master's eye had been caught by something he saw up ahead on the other side of the street.

It was Prisca, her face looking out from amid the jubilant crowd across the street.

Just as Samid spotted her, Prisca pushed her way from the crowd and ran into the middle of the road. Samid watched as she laid a large palm frond on the street with a reverent flourish—just in time for the donkey to tread upon it as Prisca lifted her head, putting her almost face-to-face with the Kind Man.

Barley let out a few quick yaps, but Prisca couldn't hear his barks over the deafening cheers. Then Barley looked back up at his master and saw he was craning his neck to catch another glimpse of Prisca. Samid even jumped up into the air a few times to try to see over taller heads, as Barley jostled about in his arms.

As the Kind Man and donkey progressed down the thoroughfare, the people lining the path behind them began to disperse. Some onlookers who were there only for the excitement walked back to the market after having glimpsed the passing curiosity. But many others—those who seemed moved by the Kind Man—began following him and his donkey down the road.

Since the crowds around them were thinning out, Samid was able to put Barley back on the ground again. After Samid stood back up, Barley heard him call to someone.

"Wait, sir . . ."

It was the funny-looking man with the smiling teeth. Barley wagged his tail.

"Yes, my friend," the man said as he stopped and turned toward Samid and Barley.

After an uncomfortable pause, Samid asked shyly, "Are there other words of the Teacher's you remember?"

The man looked at Samid, and his eyes seemed to shine.

"'Here I am! I stand at the door and knock. If anyone hears my voice and opens the door, I will come in and eat with that person, and they with me.'"

Samid looked back at the man feebly. "I don't have a door. Where I live, no one does."

The man laughed gently. Then he reached out and touched Samid's shoulder in a way Samid never allowed strangers to do. "The Teacher has told us: 'Ask and it will be given to you; seek and you will find.'"

And then he walked away.

Samid stood there for a long time while Barley waited, looking up at his master and wagging his tail. Finally, Samid scratched his beard, rubbed the bruise on his head a few times, wincing as he did, and then whistled for Barley to follow him.

D usk was settling over the city. The merchants in the marketplace were packing up their wares beneath the soft orange halo of the setting sun, which cast a magical glow over Samid and Barley as they made their way across the plaza. Samid remained lost in his thoughts and walked slowly and contemplatively, perusing various areas of the plaza searchingly.

At first Barley thought his master was looking for Prisca and Hog, so he too kept an eye out for them both. But then Barley began to sense that Samid was looking for something else. His master kept loitering near the food tables and watching the carts as they rumbled by.

Finally, Samid stopped in front of a particular bread stall. Barley couldn't understand why his master was so interested in that particular one, because it didn't emit quite as delicious an aroma as many of the others. The table was small and rickety, and the loaves were formed in simple shapes, unlike the bread from the fancier tables closer to the temple.

Samid caught the eye of the lady sitting on a stool next to the table. She was an old woman, and she sat smiling genially at the passersby.

The old baker woman stood up and said, "Very good bread. I don't go in for all the showy kinds they do today. This is just good bread, same as my mother made and her mother before that. Try? And some for your little dog?" And she broke off a piece from one of the loaves and tossed it to Barley—who was happy to get right to the business of gnawing the hard, crusty bread that was surprisingly tasty.

"Can I speak plainly?" Samid said to the woman.

And she nodded kindly.

"I am going home to a place with many hungry people. I want to try to bring them back as much food as I can. But this is all I have to spend." And Samid opened his hand and showed the old lady the coin.

"I wondered if you could try to give me as much bread as you can for this amount of money. It's not much, I know. If you can't, then I'll take what you give me. But . . . that is what I wanted to ask you."

The woman looked at him for a long time before doing anything.

Then she turned briskly and walked behind her table. From under it she took a large, rough sack. As Samid watched her, with a slight, tender grin on his face, the old woman filled the sack with as much of the bread as could fit into it.

When she was done, she lugged the sack over to Samid and put it down at his feet.

He looked at her, smiled, said nothing, and politely handed her the coin. She took it, nodded warmly, put it in the pocket of her old tunic, and then looked into Samid's eyes.

"You have journeyed a long way to get here, haven't you?"

Samid nodded yes.

"And you still have a long way to go, no?"

"Yes, I do."

"Then we'll need to be sure that—on the way—you don't lose what you've been given here today. Let me get you something to tie that sack with."

She went behind the table for a few moments, and while Samid watched Barley chew the last of the bread, the woman came back and tied the sack—good and tight—with her strong hands.

When she was done, she looked at Samid, patted him on his arm, and said, "Safe journey."

"Thank you for this," Samid replied, nodding to her politely.

"It is my gift to give," said the old woman. "Today has been a good day."

Samid picked up the sack, hoisted it onto his shoulder, and whistled for Barley to follow him. He walked away from the kind woman and into the emptying marketplace. Samid had gotten almost all the way across the plaza before he noticed that the baker woman had tied the sack with a piece of palm.

CHAPTER 10

The fire was ablaze, bellies were full. For two days now, the camp had been filled with what could almost be called joy. The people from the camp had partaken gratefully and gleefully of the food that Samid had shared freely. As Barley lay by the glowing fire, life seemed very good.

Boaz, the old flute player, was playing some of the most beautiful music Barley had ever heard. People were dancing and singing and laughing in a way that kept Barley completely delighted. The sweet noise that came out of the pipe was wordless and birdlike and soaring, and at times it filled the air with happiness. Then at other times, when

Boaz played more slowly, it made the air swirl with a beautiful sadness.

Some of the other people in the camp began to drum along with the tunes of the flute player. Not that anyone had a real drum to speak of, but they beat out rhythms with anything they could find. And all this happy and interesting noise overwhelmed Barley with a good feeling that made him wag his tail without meaning to—like his tail was trying to play music too.

Barley learned something about humans that night. When people are happy, they have their own music in them already. But when people aren't happy, then they need to make music, and when they do, even people who are poor or angry or dirty or even crazy become light and fun and free.

So that was how it was, for a good, long, and very fun couple of days in the camp. And Barley was a very happy dog. Life was good.

Above all, Barley liked watching his master be happy. And Samid—who once even danced to the music—*was* happy.

For a time.

Toward the end of the second night, the food was running low, the bread becoming scarcer and the shared pieces smaller. So, since there was little of anything left to eat, instead Samid drank.

Barley noticed that the more wine his master drank, the sadder Samid seemed to become. And soon, Samid began to say one name over and over again.

"Prisca . . ."

After two full days of revels, Samid went walking all around the camp in the middle of the night. He moved in a way Barley had never seen before—wobbling and falling, then yelling bitterly when he fell, and getting back up and wobbling again. He staggered through the camp, trying to find out if anyone had seen Prisca. The more he wandered and the more he drank, the surlier and darker he became. By dawn of the next day, not only was all the food gone, but the wine too.

After a bad night of poor sleep on the rough ground, Samid awoke, stone cold, next to where the fire had blazed the night before. Barley lay near to him, still sleeping. Samid had been in too foul a mood to amble back to his tent the night before.

"Samid . . ."

The husky whisper made Barley lift his head with a start.

"Samid . . . I have to talk to you," Hog said as he walked over toward his friend, accidentally kicking some sand onto Samid as he approached.

"Hog! You idiot!"

"Samid, I have an idea." And he plunked himself down on the ground as Samid tried to rouse himself from the head-splitting effect of days of wine.

"I spoke with Cracked Amos. A friend of his told him about a merchant's shortcut. Better than the Shepherd's Crook. It's right at the top of Old Stone Road."

"That's right in the city," Samid said, and before he even realized it, he was actually listening to what Hog was saying as he spoke in an excited whisper.

"But it's safe! That's what I'm telling you. You've been here drunk for days. You don't know what's happening. The city is tense. That teacher from Galilee has too many followers now for Rome's comfort." Hog laughed ironically. "In Judea now, it's the pious who are in danger, so they'll leave two-bit scum like us alone. And those do-gooders will get what's coming to them. Including your Prisca."

The sound of her name, spoken that way by Hog, shifted everything. "Prisca?" Samid said, his body stiffening.

Barley looked up, watching his master closely.

After a pause, Hog spoke bluntly. "She's never coming back to this camp, Samid. She's gone to follow the Galilean."

"She . . ." Samid couldn't get out any words.

"Amos saw her in town yesterday," Hog continued warily. "She bid him good-bye . . . for good."

"That can't be . . ." Samid stood up shakily. Barley stood at his side.

"Forget about her," Hog said firmly. "Come with me."

"No," said Samid. "And don't say another word about Prisca."

Hog's response was loud and firm. "Prisca has betrayed you!"

At these words, Samid stepped back on his heels in a way Barley had never seen before—a weak movement that made Barley feel a rush of panic.

"Prisca has faith in me," Samid said softly.

"Faith!" Hog howled. "You're smarter than that, Samid."

"You don't understand."

"I understand that you're shrewd enough to know that even as you shared your food with that miser Boaz, he'd have stabbed you in the eye with his flute if you reached for a crumb of the bread you'd just given him."

"Shut up!"

"You just did all that to show Prisca!"

Samid's face flushed red, and his eyes lowered to the ground. Barley could feel his master's pain. He could almost see it throbbing in the air around his master's face.

"Come with me to the city!" Hog leered into Samid's face. "By nightfall we'll have coins and food."

"No," Samid said. Then his voice suddenly splintered with emotion. "I don't want to hurt anyone anymore!"

"Oh, you're pathetic," Hog sneered. "All this piousness for love of a starry-eyed tramp . . ."

Samid roused so quickly at the sound of Hog's insult that before Hog or Barley knew what was happening, Samid had shoved Hog off his feet, pounding him down onto the charred rocks and black embers of the long-dead fire, sending up a wide puff of gray soot. Barley began to bark furiously as Hog lay there absorbing the hard fall.

"Well . . . so much for not hurting anyone."

Then Hog stood up, brushed himself off, and without looking at Samid again turned away and said loudly into the dawning morning, "I was your friend."

Samid stood clutching his head as he stared after Hog's retreating figure. After a few moments, he wobbled to his feet. Overwhelmed by the pain of his wine-soaked mind, he now focused his anger on the only thing nearby to be blamed.

"Stop barking!"

It was the way Samid screamed these two words that shocked Barley into silence—the hatred in his master's eyes, the rage in his voice, the disdain that twisted his face.

Barley looked up at his master—not wagging, just blinking.

"You stay!" Samid yelled over his shoulder as he stormed off toward his tent and disappeared into it.

Barley didn't know if he should follow his master.

He always had.

Barley trotted up to the tent. He peered in. Samid was

now lying facedown on his pillow. Barley walked into the tent timidly and quietly assumed his usual position on the pile of dirty clothing that was his little bed. Once Barley lay down, he let out an involuntary sigh that whistled softly through the nostrils of his tiny black nose.

And Samid heard it.

Wildly, Samid pushed himself up off his pillow, wheeled around, and, seeing Barley comfortably atop his clothes, flew toward him in anger.

"I had told you to stay! Get out!"

Barley stood up, his legs ambling slowly, his head dropping deep down into his shoulders. With his belly an inch from the ground, Barley crawled slowly out of the tent.

He looked back over his shoulder once before he lay down just outside of his master's tent, his stomach pressed against the hard desert dirt.

S amid awoke gradually, emerging from the depths of a fitful sleep, to the high-pitched cries of his dog.

"Boy . . . !"

Samid leapt up from his pillow and flew out of the tent, hurling his body in the direction of Barley's howls.

And so it was in this state that he was greeted by the sight of Barley giving a heartfelt greeting to Prisca.

Samid paused, catching his breath, and after a few moments, he smiled.

So did Prisca.

"Sleeping outside on such a cold night?" she said, looking at Barley. But clearly her words were meant for Samid.

Soon the three of them were sitting huddled together in Samid's tent. Prisca had brought them a gift—a small piece of bread the size of a child's fist. She and Samid and Barley split it three ways. Samid, in his contrition, gave Barley a human-size share. And Samid had a small gift of his own to add to the evening. From under a small pile of grubby trinkets in the corner of his tent, he produced the stub of a candle he had once retrieved from a garbage pile. The lowly candle stub was enough to light up the tent with a comforting glow.

Samid and Prisca talked and talked as Barley situated himself comfortably between them. Barley began to doze peacefully while Prisca looked down at him and petted him.

"He looks like a little lamb."

The soft, comforting sound of Prisca's and Samid's murmuring voices gave Barley a feeling of home.

"I was never going to come back here—ever again," Prisca said as Samid listened intently. "I have only heard the Teacher speak a few times. But after seeing him on Sunday and looking into his eyes as I laid a palm in his path, I made up my mind to follow him. And to never come back to this place again."

Samid's eyes fell away from Prisca's face.

"But then . . . it was uncanny . . . Two days ago, while watching with many of the Teacher's followers, I saw something . . . with my own eyes."

"What did you see, Prisca?"

"That merchant from the other day, the one who hit you—you remember him."

"Remember him?" Samid huffed. "I still have the welt from his whip on my hand."

"Samid, with my own eyes, I saw the Teacher walk into the temple, pick up another merchant's whip, and lash it across a tableful of coins, sending them clanging and echoing across the temple floor."

"This Teacher did that in the temple?" Samid said, amazed. "Then he must be a madman."

"What's more, I saw him walk up to the very merchant who had hit you. The man was sitting puffed up and perched on a cushioned chair—like a king—selling his captive birds, right in the temple. The Teacher went over to that very man, pulled the chair out from under him, and swung it at the door to the cage, freeing those doves to soar through the temple and out of the door to daylight!"

There was silence, then Samid said, "This Teacher of yours did that, Prisca? To that man?"

"He did." Prisca nodded soberly. "To the very man who hurt you!"

Samid scratched his beard and remained silent for a few moments.

Prisca's eyes began to fill with tears as she continued. "This Teacher from Galilee is the only reason I've been able to let go of something that has held me in one sad place for so long—an endless, joy-wrecking, unforgiving . . ."

"Despair."

Samid said the word before she could. Which made them smile at each other, sweetly but sadly.

"Why is our despair such a difficult thing for us to give up?" asked Samid.

Prisca replied, "I think despair is so difficult to let go of because it helps us to justify the worst things inside of us. We think: I lack, so I can steal. I hurt, so I can injure. I failed at one thing, so now watch me destroy my whole life . . . But when the despair is gone, we cannot help but change. We simply must."

The two were silent for a few moments.

Barley, who had been lulled to sleep by the gentle waves of their conversation, stirred from his napping just enough to twist his body over onto his back to solicit a stomach rub.

"Like this little one," Prisca laughed. "He doesn't despair," she said, rubbing Barley's belly. "He's always looking for the next good thing. A hand to lick, some food to chomp, a stick to fetch, a sight to see, a friend to curl up next to."

"The next good thing . . ." Samid said softly.

Now Prisca's tone changed as she spoke purposefully. "Tomorrow evening," she said in a serious whisper, "some of us will be meeting. Those who believe. It's a secret place, in the city. We're not to bring anyone that the whole group is not expecting. But I'll tell them about you tonight. And you can meet us at sundown tomorrow."

But Samid's expression was uneasy.

Prisca stated frankly, "It could be dangerous. So I'll understand if you don't come."

Before Samid could respond, Prisca took her finger and drew a map of the secret place, tracing the path in the dirt floor of Samid's tent.

Soon, Prisca gave Barley a farewell pat and took her leave for the evening. Samid and Barley followed her out of the tent and watched as she crossed the field. They turned back to their own tent only when she had safely entered the tent she shared with some women of the camp.

"C'mon, boy," Samid said, cocking his head toward the inside of the tent.

But Barley didn't move.

Barley looked up at Samid, tilting his head to one side with a confused and slightly fearful look.

Samid crouched down, eye level with his dog, and let out a slow, mellow whistle, to which Barley responded with a slow, hesitant walk over to his master. Then Samid reached out, cupped his hand under Barley's snout, and looked into his dog's eyes.

"I'm sorry I was mean to you, Boy."

Barley wagged his tail.

"C'mon."

And they both started toward the tent.

"Sam-did . . . !"

The voice came out of the darkness, low and raspy.

Samid stood up straight. This voice in the night made him jump.

"Hog? Is that you?"

Samid peered into the shadows. Boaz—his flute in one hand, his hat made of rags in the other—was walking toward him.

"Boaz. 'Evening."

Boaz stopped and stood close to Samid, with Barley below, looking up at them both.

"Sam-did," Boaz said, the way he always mispronounced his name. "You gave bread . . ."

"Yes," Samid nodded, "the other night . . ."

"Today," Boaz told him, "I play . . . in city."

And with a toothless grin, he added, "Beauuuuutifully," as if the word itself was a song.

"I'm sure you did." Samid smiled.

"Look," Boaz said, and showed his upturned rag-hat to Samid. "I get!"

Samid looked down and saw three coins in the hat.

"Oh, Boaz!" Samid patted his shoulder. "Well done!"

Boaz reached his gnarled hands into the hat. He took out one of the coins and handed it to Samid.

"For you, Sam-did."

Samid paused for a moment. Then he reached out, took the coin, closed it into his hand, and grinned, saying humbly, "Thank you," as Boaz reached his hand down to Barley, who softly licked the old flute player's knuckles.

CHAPTER 11

Barley stayed so close by his master's heel, his rope-leash hung slack in Samid's hand for most of their midday journey to the city. The air of the oncoming dusk was brisk, and the end-of-day smells of the city were nice to sniff as they wafted past Barley on the wind of early night. Samid was deep in thought as he led Barley through the quieting streets to the place where Prisca had told him to meet.

They were now on a hilly road that led down to a marketplace. Though Samid had an idle realization they were on "Old Stone Road," he had no intention of stopping till he felt Barley tug, then halt, then stare across the road.

Samid glanced toward the hilltop and saw near a thicket of bushes the massive boulder that gave the street its name. And sticking up over the top of that boulder: a familiar, fat head.

"Idiot!" Samid said under his breath as he watched. Hog was on tiptoes, peering over the boulder toward the market below, nervously awaiting an unsuspecting merchant to pass by his clever hiding place. So clever a hiding place he had no clue he was being stared at by a tall man and a tail-wagging dog. "Idiot," Samid laughed again to Barley, as Barley wagged in what seemed like agreement. But Samid stopped laughing the second he heard the voice of a man and woman coming up the hill, a husband and wife, two merchants.

"Hello, friends!"

Hog's figure emerged from behind the large tree, his tone friendly, his face smiling. The buoyant energy of his greeting took the couple by surprise, but the toothy grin on his wide, moonish face and the charm he sang into his tone disarmed the couple, and they smiled back warmly.

"I see you are merchants! You must know the city well. Could you perhaps give a lost traveler directions to where I am going?"

"Of course, sir," the lady said as the man nodded obligingly.

Samid's voice boomed through the air.

"Merchants! Step away from that odd-shaped man, if you know what's good for you!"

A startled Hog turned toward the sound of Samid's voice.

Samid could not help but grin at Hog's immense shock and at the blank stares of the merchants.

Samid announced loudly, "That fellow means to do you both harm!"

"What?" gasped the merchant, taking a step back from Hog and pulling his wife behind him.

"Yes! He's a very bad man. Blubbery of belly and hard of heart!" Samid said melodramatically, quite enjoying his own performance.

Hog tried to speak. "Bu . . . I . . . You . . . Sami . . . I . . . wha . . ." Articulate as always, and now in the throes of rage.

"Why, just last week I saw that round-shaped thug beat a poor baker bloody just to get his thieving fingers on"—his voice rising—"the same sort of coin purse that you, sir, are no doubt carrying!"

"*What?*" the wife shrieked.

"Oh!" the man gasped as he clutched his coin purse.

"Samid, you rat!" Hog gurgled, choking in his fury.

Samid screamed to the bug-eyed couple, "Get away from him! Run for your lives!" And as the couple grabbed for each other and began to flee, Samid emptied his lungs. "Gooooo!"

And go they did!

The couple ran down the road as fast as they could, the man clutching his coin purse with both hands.

Samid called out to them, "And warn anyone coming up the road! His name is Hog!"

And with that, the frantic couple rounded the corner at the bottom of the street and were gone.

By now Samid was laughing so loud that his chest heaved with a mirth he had not succumbed to since he was a child. He threw back his head and aimed his big, low chuckles up to the heavens as Barley stood beside him wagging his tail and looking up into his master's face.

All Hog could do was sputter, "You . . . you . . . you . . . you . . . !"

Samid got hold of himself and walked over to Hog. Samid spoke in a tone of sincerity and even with a touch of affection.

"Hog, I couldn't let you do this."

"What business is it of yours, you rat, weasel, you snake, you . . . you . . . you . . . ?"

"You said to me last night that you are my friend, Hog. And you are. The reason we have friends is so that there's someone around to save us from ourselves."

Then Samid bent down and took the rope from around

Barley's neck, allowing him to go free, sure he was going to do exactly what he did, which was dash over to Hog, a familiar face, and give him a big greeting. Barley ran to Hog and hopped up with his front paws happily tapping on Hog's belly. But Hog was in no mood for the affection of a dog, or for talk about being friends with the rat who just ruined his perfect plan to get money for food. He pushed Barley off of him and growled at Samid, "I give you this for your friendship!" and spat onto the ground.

Samid shook his head with finality and emotion. "No more, Hog. No more hurting people. No more taking things that are not ours. No more mischief."

Then he clapped his arm good-naturedly around Hog's back and said, smiling, "Come, my funny-looking friend, we're getting out of here," and he began leading Hog down the street—Samid strolling, Hog resisting, and Barley following right along, happily.

After a few paces, Hog pulled away.

"No! I'm not going with you!"

"Yes, you are. I won't let you stay here and do this sort of thing anymore. You're coming with me. Or . . ." Samid took the bunched-up rope in his hand, held it in front of Hog's face, and said, "Or, if need be, I'll put this leash around your fat head and drag you with me," closing the deal by bopping him on the nose with the rope.

Then Samid put his arm around Hog, pulling him into

an affectionate choke, and walked him down the road, with Hog squirming and huffing and complaining as they went. "I think you've gotten more cracked than Cracked Amos!"

Samid replied, "I'll explain as we walk. I'm going to buy you some breakfast. And some lunch. Come on."

"Buy me food? How can you buy me food?" Hog shook his head in misery and said sadly, "Samid . . . I'm hungry. I'm so hungry. You have nothing. I have nothing. And I'm so tired of having nothing."

Samid could see over Hog's shoulder that two merchants were coming up over the hill. One was an older man with a turban who walked with a slight limp, and the other was a much younger woman, who Samid took to be the man's daughter, who had long, flowing black hair and was talking softly.

Hog turned and looked up the road.

Samid said quickly, "Hog, I have something for you."

"What?"

"Money," Samid answered, grinning broadly.

Hog spun back around to him.

"What?"

"Yes! Money! A coin . . ."

"Where did you get it?"

"From Boaz the flute player."

"You stole it from that old tightwad?"

"No, Hog, he gave it to me!"

"Boaz the flute player gave you a coin?"

Samid laughed. "Yes! He did! To thank me for buying him bread!"

The two of them began to walk together down the street as Samid reached into his tunic. "He gave it to me," Samid said, "and now I give it to you. Here." And he handed the coin to Hog.

Hog looked at the coin, and his face fell in disappointment.

"Some coin. That won't get me much."

"No, my lumpy friend, but it's a beginning. You know what your problem is, Hog?" Samid said as they walked.

"What?"

"Despair."

As they walked down the road, a song suddenly filled the morning air. It was the daughter of the merchant singing as she strolled down the road with her father. The song was exotic and haunting and beautiful, unfurling in syllables that lifted melodically into the rosy dawn.

"See," Samid said. "You've got a coin in your pocket, a song to send us on our way, a pretty sky to walk under, and friends, just like a family out on a happy Sunday."

"It's Thursday, you dolt."

Samid laughed as he patted his friend's back.

Hog laughed too. "Some family," he said with a reluctant grin. Then, seeing a stick in the road, Hog picked it up and tossed it down the road with a chuckle.

Barley trotted down the road happily, chasing the stick.

"Hey, Samid," Hog said from behind him.

Samid turned around to answer. When he did, his lip was struck by the coin Hog had thrown with all his strength at Samid's face. The small, hard chunk of metal stunned Samid with a jolt of pain and shock.

"Fool!" Hog laughed out the word gleefully, sealing his betrayal.

As he backed away swiftly from Samid, he taunted him, "To blazes with you, you weak, pathetic fool."

Then Hog took off down the road toward the old merchant and his daughter, moving as fast as his hunger and his rage would take him.

"Hog, come back here."

Samid turned and called to Barley, who was trotting back to lay the stick by his master's foot. Samid bent down quickly and put the rope back around Barley's neck. With a sharp "C'mon," the two of them took off running up the road toward Hog and the merchants, Barley now sensing his master's intensity.

Hog had moved his lumbering body up the street as swiftly as he could without making the two merchants suspicious, as he called ahead to them, "Oh, how fortunate to find two kind citizens! I was wondering if you might direct a lost traveler . . ."

Samid cupped his free hand at the side of his mouth and hollered up the street as he ran with Barley, "Sir! Lady! That man means to rob you! Run!"

But the old man just peered down the road at Samid and smiled.

So Samid began to wave his arms wildly at the merchants and, running as fast as he could, yelled out, "He will hurt you, sir!"

But the old man just waved back to Samid cheerily and through a toothless smile intoned a kindly flow of words—every one of which, Samid now knew, was in a foreign tongue.

Hog pounced.

He swung his beefy leg hard and swept the old man's spindly shins out from under him, dropping him into the street. As the old man landed in a heap, the daughter burst into a ferocious chorus of high-pitched wails and foreign words.

When he saw the chaos ahead, Samid stopped abruptly, and Barley skidded to comply.

Samid looked around desperately until his eyes fell on what he needed—a thin, sturdy tree at the side of the road.

He yanked the rope, and Barley followed his master to the tree. Samid crouched down and tied the free end of Barley's rope to the tree as tightly as he could.

"I don't want you to get hurt again, boy. I'll be right back."

Then Samid took off, dashing up the road as fast as his long strides would carry him, the rhythmic pounding of his sandals on the road drowned out by the earsplitting howls of the man's daughter. Barley watched with mounting anxiousness, moving forward until the rope halted him. Then he backpedaled and began to prance in place, bobbing his head and letting out a loud mix of sharp barks and glum yowls as he watched the scene up the road.

Hog had wasted no time in finding the fallen merchant's coin purse and was now trying to yank it off the old man's belt, elated to find such an easy victim. But easy victims sometimes know they're easy and thus go out into the world equipped. From deep inside the front folds of her flowing and exotically colored robe, the daughter pulled a thin, shiny blade.

Hog was bent over the father and had just pulled the purse hard enough that it ripped off the man's belt, spilling coins. Hog felt triumphant, unaware that behind him, a wild-eyed, blade-wielding daughter was heading toward him with the intent of stabbing her father's attacker in the heart.

The moment Samid saw the telltale gleam of the blade,

he gasped and, without breaking stride, bellowed up the road. "Hooooooggg!"

Samid yelled with such uncharacteristic desperation that even Hog had to turn round to see what the commotion was about.

While Hog did not turn in time to avoid the oncoming blade completely, he did move his massive body enough that the path to his heart the daughter aimed for was avoided, and her knife found only the edge of Hog's tunic, shredding a slice of it and exposing his large, pink middle.

The daughter persisted.

She wheeled back around toward Hog, coming at him again, screaming and plunging her thin arm down to stab her father's attacker. But Hog caught her by the wrist.

By the time Samid got to them, Hog and the daughter were rocking to and fro in mortal conflict over control of the blade, each hollering in a different tongue. Samid simply reached in and, with one deft grab-and-twist, snapped the blade away from them. As Samid stepped back so that neither could grab it again, Hog pushed the woman hard, sending her flying back several feet and landing in the street.

Down the road Barley barked more frantically than before, a husky, primal call that rattled Samid and added to his impatience when Hog came back at him.

Hog lunged at Samid, reaching wildly for the knife. For

a while Samid just stood tall and still, holding the weapon safely behind his back, keeping Hog at bay and watching him flail ridiculously, until finally he had had enough.

Samid punched Hog in the face—a shot to the jaw that dropped Hog to the street.

He leaned over his former friend's felled body and said, "That was for your own good."

With Hog and the wailing daughter both dazed, Samid attended to the old man who lay on the street, moaning a sad stream of unintelligible words. Crouching down, Samid helped him into a sitting position. Then he handed the torn coin purse back to the man and began to gather up the coins, putting the knife in his teeth as he scooped them up from the road.

When the man saw that Samid was there to help him and not hurt him, he began to cry and kiss Samid repeatedly on his arms and on the hem of his grubby tunic.

The man's daughter had, by this time, gotten up off the ground and was now swatting at Hog, who was just getting back onto his feet after Samid's punch. As Hog struggled to get his balance, the woman clawed at his jowly face and screamed. He positioned his legs in a wide stance and then, with a loud, strength-summoning grunt, pushed the woman out of his face and onto her back, flattening her again onto the street.

As Hog raised his head victoriously, he found himself looking straight into the red eyes of a massive, charging horse.

Before Hog's face had time to register fear, the Roman soldier on the horse had driven his sword so far into Hog's torso that the momentum carried his speared body several gallops before it fell in the street. Without stopping, the soldier pulled the sword from Hog, drawing forth a cascade of terrible red that Barley saw ooze over Hog's limp body as horse and rider sped up the road, heading straight toward Barley's master.

Samid froze. He did not move even as the powerful horse, reined by the huge rider, skidded to a stop inches in front of him.

Samid raised his head slowly to see that he was staring at the point of the soldier's sword, still dripping with Hog's blood.

Now the rider, clad in Roman armor, looked down to survey the scene.

Samid looked up at the soldier.

"I . . . I was trying to help . . ."

"Yes. I see that," the soldier's low voice boomed back. "Trying to help yourself to this merchant's money."

"Is this *your* coin purse?" the soldier asked the old man, pointing with his sword. The old man nodded yes.

The soldier smiled with satisfaction and said, "Some merchants coming down the street said there was a robber up the road, and it looks like they were right."

Now the daughter ran over to her father, crying hysterically.

"Quiet!" the soldier yelled.

Then he maneuvered the giant horse even closer to Samid and sneered, "Don't worry, I'll take care of this one."

As the daughter bent down to gather up the coin purse and help her father stand, the soldier looked down at Samid and ordered loudly, "Stand up!"

Samid stood, and in one expert motion, the soldier whipped out a rope that landed around Samid's neck. The rope was tied into a thick noose.

As soon as the rope landed on his master's neck, Barley made a desperately sad yelp that Samid had never heard him make before. Samid turned away from Barley sadly.

Seeing what the soldier had done to Samid, the old man reacted passionately.

He began to protest to the soldier, repeating a phrase in his language over and over, the same handful of syllables uttered pleadingly as the man began to cry through his words—words that neither the soldier nor Samid knew or understood, words meant to tell the soldier Samid was not a bad man.

When the soldier failed to understand his meaning, the man even reached up and tried to take the noose from Samid's neck.

The soldier swiped his sword down at the man.

"Don't interfere with me! Are you too ignorant to know when a soldier is trying to help you? Go!"

Terrified by the soldier's tone, the daughter grabbed her father and the coin purse and, leaving her knife lying in the street, they hurried off in the same direction they had come from.

The soldier leered at Samid. "Well, well, well . . . Found you just in time."

Samid kept his back turned to Barley.

He thought it best to.

Barley raised his eyes, his head still lowered, and two large crescents of white formed under his brown pupils. He wanted his master to look at him.

But his master wouldn't. Even when Barley began to cry—his small black nose pulsating feebly with high-pitched whimpers—his master did not turn around.

The soldier gave a sharp snap of the reins, ordered, "Let's go!" and, gritting his teeth in a hateful scowl, clutched the rope hard as Samid reached up to try to get his fingers between the rope and his throat, at least enough to let him breathe. Then the soldier used his other hand to expertly maneuver the reins of the huge horse, turning him around sharply. As the horse turned, Samid was yanked with such force that, for a second, both his feet were swept off the ground. And in this way, they started down the road.

Barley's thin, airy cries quickened as he watched his master be taken away down the street.

Just as they were at the bottom of the hill, about to round the bend of the road, Samid craned his head back and peered over his shoulder to take one last look at his dog.

And then he was gone.

Though the road was now empty, Barley could not take his eyes off the vacant turn around which his master had disappeared. He stood still, even as the heavy weight of sadness began to lower his body, first into a crouch, then down onto his belly, where he lay in the street and kept staring at the empty spot, staring unblinkingly at nothing at all.

Then—! There it was!

Barley sprang back up, eyes wide, tail up, paws poised. Yes! He knew it for certain. Though far off now, it was unmistakable.

His master's whistle.

CHAPTER 12

It was Barley's instinct to run after his master, to follow his call. So he did. But his hind legs slid from under him as the rope that was ringing his neck yanked him back.

Barley stood up, walked back till the rope was slack again. He coughed twice, then stood there, stock-still. He couldn't follow, run, or help. All Barley could do was bark. He barked across the road at the stone-still body of Hog. But Hog was no help.

The sky began to darken as Barley continued to bark. After a while, Barley's barking deepened into a hopeless howl, and darkness covered the road.

Barley barked and howled until his voice was hoarse

with the effort. He stopped and remained quiet for long, empty minutes, the realization sinking in that his master was gone. Through the bleak, silent darkness, Barley thought he began to sense something or someone approaching.

It began as a very far-off *clah-clink, clah-clink, clah-clink*, a rhythmic clanking of metal that grew louder as it neared, coming from the direction in which his master had been taken.

As the sound grew closer, Barley could hear that the sound was a strange kind of half growling, half singing.

The small gray slice of moon was no match for the dank mist, so Barley knew that by the time he could get a good look at whatever was coming near, it would almost be upon him.

Within the low droning, Barley heard another sound, a thumping accompaniment to the eerie tune that Barley recognized. It was the sound of a horse's hooves trotting on the road. A large horse, by the sound of it. And Barley finally began to recognize the figure of a man mounted atop the horse. The man was singing an agonizing song.

Barley stood waiting for the arrival of the horse and man making this strange music.

As the party drew very close to where Barley stood tied to the tree, Barley could discern that the man had a helmet. The helmet was not on his head but was hanging awkwardly on a hook on his horse's rein. The man's cape was askew, and he was drinking out of a wineskin. Barley could sense the rank smell of the strong drink that permeated the man's sweaty body.

The man was a soldier. And he was drunk.

As soon as he saw Barley, the soldier stopped his singing.

Barley peered at him, shaking in silence.

The soldier spoke in a slurred, guttural voice that cut through the quiet.

"Cur? A mangy cur? How nice!"

The horrible sound echoed through the street in what sounded like something between laughter and screaming.

"Now I'll—"

And interrupting his own drunken words, the man slid off the horse, landing on the road with such a thud that Barley saw a great cloud of dirt rise from the man's heavy boots and waft up his large body.

Then the soldier straightened himself to his full height and stood there. To Barley he looked every bit as big and solid as the boulder he was cowering near.

The soldier exhaled a rumbling groan. "I'll show you how we can fix the little ones, like you, that need fixing!"

With a forceful heave he drew his sword.

The soldier moved toward Barley, gripping his sword tightly and pointing at Barley's little body as Barley cowered. Once his belly, and then his face, had touched the ground, Barley closed his eyes and pressed his little head as firmly as he could into the dirt below him.

Then it came.

The terrible jolt.

A terrific force ran through Barley's throat, filled his head with an echoing rip, shook his spine, and upended his entire body.

And then—nothing.

After a few seconds, Barley opened his eyes. He saw the soldier staggering back toward his horse. Intuitively, Barley stood up. As soon as he did, he looked down and saw on the ground the rope from his neck, sliced cleanly in two.

Barley looked up at the man in astonishment as the soldier climbed back onto his horse, downed a huge swig of wine, looked over at Barley with a smile, and said, "That'll fix you, little boy. Run free."

Then, picking up his song right where he left off, the soldier gave his horse a yank and began to trot away, singing off into the night.

B arley roved long stretches of road, his keen eyes peering through the faintly moonlit distance and glancing down side roads and alleyways as he made his way.

He had traveled a good distance in the thickest darkness

before reaching a place within the city walls where he saw an unmistakable orange glow lighting up the low clouds. The glow was emanating from a large fire under a garden of trees behind a high iron fence. Barley saw the silhouettes of people warming themselves as the blaze flickered. He could tell they were all men, about a dozen of them, and Barley could hear they were talking and laughing.

Pushing against the harsh wind, Barley sidled along the fence until he saw an opening, a gate that was ajar with room for him to slip in. Barley scooted through the gate and trotted slowly toward the fire, getting as close as he could without being noticed. He stopped, looked around, and could see by the light of the fire that he was in a large fenced area next to a mammoth building that seemed to stretch as far as his eyes could see in each direction. As he looked more closely at the men around the fire, their faces no longer in silhouette, Barley could see who they were.

The men were all Roman soldiers.

They were chuckling gruffly and passing wineskins between them. Their heavy helmets lay at their sides, their capes bunched on the ground where the men sprawled, their metal weapons propped up near the fire, making crisscross shapes against the illuminated sky.

Barley turned and launched himself forward toward the gate, but before he could pass through it, he heard a clamorous sound rising from the path he had just followed through the gate. It was the sound of pounding hooves.

Barley stopped and stood still, watching with his ears pinned back as the horses came up the hill—huge horses mounted with soldiers, some of them holding fiery torches, others wearing shiny armor and capes with extra flourishes of fabric or silver plating. Another cluster of men followed the mounted soldiers on foot.

The moment these new soldiers arrived, the ones by the fire reacted with haste. In a moment, all wineskins were hurled aside, helmets were clapped back onto heads, capes were straightened, and the men snapped themselves into a formal military line and stood erect—in a flash, each man a model of duty and respectability.

Barley saw these arriving soldiers were leaders—severe men with strict discipline who passed through the gate with no acknowledgment of the other soldiers who were standing respectfully. They headed toward the big building as Barley trotted along the wall several paces until he was safely in the shadows, where he sat to watch the commotion and wait for it to die down.

Once the group of soldiers reached the wall, the riders on horseback dismounted and stood waiting with the foot soldiers in a tight cluster. Then, after some echoing clangs, a heavy door in the wall of the big building was pushed open from within. The soldiers began to enter the building, and as the tight cluster of soldiers broke apart, Barley saw someone he recognized at the center of the group.

It was the Kind Man.

Barley was surprised to see him, but very glad.

The Kind Man's light garments gave off a dim glow amid the sea of soldiers' red uniforms. Barley felt so happy to see the Kind Man again that he began to wag his tail excitedly.

The last time Barley had seen the Kind Man was when he was riding the donkey and the citizens had pushed their way to the front of the crowd to lay down the large green leaves and blanket the Kind Man's way.

Tonight there were no palms, no cheering crowds.

Tonight a few soldiers were walking alongside the Kind Man and holding on to him tightly, roughly. And the soldiers' faces were cold and serious, unlike the citizens who greeted the Kind Man as he entered the city on the donkey and were so full of joy at seeing him.

But one thing that hadn't changed since the last time Barley had seen the Kind Man was the look on his face.

He seemed just as kind as ever.

His expression was peaceful, his eyes soft and glistening, his head held with sincerity and poise. And Barley could feel the same warm feeling coming from the Kind Man's eyes that he had felt the first time he saw him. Tonight the people who were around the Kind Man were acting differently, but the Kind Man seemed just as interesting and beautiful and kind to Barley as he had before.

Barley watched as the soldiers ushered the Kind Man through the door and he disappeared into the building, followed by the rest of the soldiers. Then, with a solid thud and a series of loud clangs, the huge door was shut and locked.

Barley turned and saw that the gate to the fence behind him, through which the soldiers had just come, was also shut and locked.

Barley was alone.

He barked twice.

Barley looked up anxiously at the door into which the Kind Man had been taken. He stood watching the door for a few moments.

Then Barley began to look around at his surroundings—the darkness around him, the tall trees and the fence. He could feel that the trimmed grass under his paws was thick and soft. Once he found a spot he liked, Barley laid his belly on the ground, keeping his head up. He did not turn around three times and curl himself into a ball to go to sleep, like he usually did.

Barley did not want to go to sleep tonight.

CHAPTER 13

The following day, the dawn brought with it ominous weather that seemed strange and felt wrong.

Usually in this desert region the nights were windy, raw, and cold—until the sun of morning warmed the day into an eventual bright blaze of noon. But this day was different. The weather the night before had been balmy and genial, and Barley had passed a pleasant watch, sitting there awake and alert until daybreak in a breath-warm breeze. But when dawn came, it brought with it a silver sky filled with leaden clouds and gusts of unpredictable wind that blew away the warmth of the previous night and left an icy dampness in the Friday air.

Through the night, Barley had heard strange commotions, arrivals and departures on the other side of the large stone wall. But he never saw anyone arrive or depart again from the door that he watched all night. So Barley spent the morning continuing to watch, even though the grass was damp with cold morning dew and the wind was strong.

Barley stayed where he was, as close as he could get to his master and to the Kind Man.

Barley kept hearing a noise, a sound he couldn't quite place. It sounded to Barley almost as though the lower part of the sky was whispering—softly, but in anger. As Barley listened, he could not make out any specific human voice in the sound, but he heard something in it that had a vaguely human rhythm to it. Soon, he realized what the sound was. It was the loud sound of many voices.

A crowd was forming around the side of the giant building. The last crowd Barley had heard making this sort of collective noise had gathered to see the Kind Man when he came into Jerusalem. Now that he heard the same noise—a roar of many voices off in the distance—he began to worry that maybe the Kind Man was with a crowd again, and he was not there to see him.

Barley ran frantically around the fenced yard along the

side of the building, searching for a way to escape. Finally, he found it—a small dip in the ground beneath the fence just large enough for Barley to squeeze his small body through.

Once he was free, Barley ran for a long time toward the sound of the crowd. At last he saw stretching before him a massive plaza—not quite as large as the temple marketplace but much colder and statelier. The plaza was filled with soldiers—dozens of them—all with their backs to Barley, looking forward at a procession of people forming at the far end of the plaza. Several wide stairs descended to the street where the crowd had gathered. The street-level noise was now surging over the wide steps and echoing off the buildings in the vast plaza. Barley ran across the plaza and made his way down onto the street.

Barley could see that the people at the head of the crowd had begun to move up the street at the bottom of the plaza steps and were now making the first turn up one of the many winding roads that wove through that part of the city.

Barley looked around him for a break in the thronging mass of people. He cocked his head alertly in all directions, searching for a path, until finally his eyes fell on a promising sight.

Barley looked at the looming chain of stone structures bordering the crowded street. The buildings rose up at the same steep angle as the incline of the street they fronted.

Barley noticed one building in particular near the crest of the hill toward which the crowd progressed. He saw a bit of daylight shining between it and the building next to it—a small alleyway. Barley could see through that slender opening a sliver of the huge crowd lining the sides of the street and looking back down the road toward the plaza.

Barley had found his shortcut.

He saw that he could snake his way up to the backs of those buildings by climbing one small wall that led up the hill, then all he had to do was scamper up a small patch of hillside ground that led up to the alleyway. From there he could get to the head of the procession.

Barley turned from the crowd and made for the wall that would be the first step in his trek. Barley anticipated the wall's height and leapt through the air in one arcing jump, landing atop the wall. He scooted along the length of its narrow edge until he reached the patch of rocky cliffside that now separated him from the alleyway leading to the street.

In a moment, Barley was quickly up the cliff and running into the little alley. He easily fit through its narrow length and soon found himself at the top of the crowded street.

The street was lined with so many people that Barley's view of it was obscured. He pushed into the crowd, making his way through a gauntlet of legs, until he reached the street's edge. From this vantage point, he had a clear view of the procession coming up the street.

Barley waited and watched. While this crowd looked similar to the crowd that had gathered the last time he had seen the Kind Man, the feeling in the air was very different.

This time there was no jubilation. There was a whiff of danger in the air that made Barley uneasy. The mood of this crowd was as ugly as the ashen sky and hissing clouds overhead.

As Barley looked down the hill to the bottom of the street, he could tell by the way the crowd was shuffling, pointing, reacting, craning necks, and standing up on tiptoes that the procession was just now rounding the curve to walk up the road.

Then Barley saw him, at the center of an angry escort of soldiers pushing through the crowd.

It was the Kind Man.

Even at a distance, Barley recognized his eyes— unmistakable and beautiful.

But everything else about the Kind Man looked different now.

He was not wearing the clean white cloak that seemed to glow when Barley saw it shining in the sun and hanging gracefully off the Kind Man's tall, thin frame. Now, all the Kind Man had on his body was a torn red cloak—draped awkwardly over his back and hanging down over some tattered undergarments tied loosely around his waist. And somehow his frame looked even thinner than it had just hours before when Barley had seen him with the soldiers.

And Barley saw that he was carrying an enormous piece of wood.

This confused Barley.

It looked to him like the Kind Man did not want to be carrying the wood, like it was hurting him and making him distressed. Barley wondered why he didn't just put down the wood in the street and walk without it. But the Kind Man didn't. He kept carrying the heavy wood up the incline of the road, wincing and sweating as he worked to keep it on his shoulders as he climbed the stone street.

The crossbar he was carrying was so large and so rough-hewn that even from far up the street, Barley could see its coarse, splintery surface cutting into the Kind Man's back and shoulders. It was so heavy it weighed the Kind Man down so that he could only walk slowly, one unsure step followed by the next.

As the Kind Man moved up the road, closer to where Barley stood, Barley could see that his back and arms had several long, red marks on them, like the marks Duv carved into wood and painted to make his beautiful birds. But the marks on the Kind Man's body were not beautiful to Barley.

The Kind Man continued up the road slowly, shifting the heavy wood and struggling with each step. He was trying to keep moving, pausing every few seconds to summon strength from deep inside his bent body to continue making his way up the road.

When the Kind Man moved within feet of Barley, Barley realized he could not see the man's long hair. The Kind Man's hair was being held back by something encircling his head.

It looked to Barley like a shattered wooden water bowl, an ugly basket, or the nest of a terrible bird had been placed atop the Kind Man's head. When the Kind Man came closer still to Barley's spot along the road, Barley finally realized what it was.

It was no bowl or basket or nest encircling the Kind Man's head.

It was thorns

The thorns were long and sharp and scary to look at, and they were pressing into the Kind Man's forehead and scalp.

Nobody from the crowd moved forward to help the Kind Man. They just stood and watched as he lugged the heavy wood up the hill, with thorns wreathing his head in a mangle of punctures.

Now Barley began to notice something about the Kind Man's legs, which were at Barley's eye level. They were quivering. The weight of the wood was bearing down on the Kind Man's torso and lower limbs until, after a few more strained steps, they began to wobble awkwardly. The Kind Man stood in place for one teetering second. Then his body collapsed, dropping down onto the street as the crowd gasped loudly. The huge piece of wood followed immediately, landing with a loud crack and then a thud—half on the street, half across the Kind Man's back.

For a few seconds, there was a numb pause, and the crowd hushed as the Kind Man lay in the road, dazed and weak, his chest flat on the ground. Then some in the crowd became impatient at the lull in the procession, and this feeling rippled through the crowd until a few citizens actually shouted for him to get back up. At this, the Kind Man lifted his head weakly and with a look of such deep sadness that Barley could begin to see it, for the first time, overtaking the kindness of his eyes.

But just as Barley began to feel despair over what he was witnessing, he glimpsed what seemed to be a ray of goodness from one of the soldiers.

As soon as the Kind Man fell, this soldier immediately

ran to the Kind Man's side. Barley watched as the soldier lifted the heavy wood off the Kind Man's back and let it drop next to him in the street.

Once the Kind Man's back was clear of the fallen wood, the soldier lifted what Barley saw was a whip and began swinging it down onto the fallen man again and again, the earsplitting cracks ringing out each time the soldier's whip landed.

Now Barley understood that the soldier had not moved the wood off the Kind Man's back to help him. He also now understood how the Kind Man came to have those long, red marks on his body.

Barley cowered as he watched the soldier beat the Kind Man, his body wincing at the landing of each lash.

At long last, the Kind Man pushed himself up off the ground, even amid the onslaught of the whip. As he did, the soldier lifted the wood back up onto the Kind Man's bloody shoulders, and the procession continued.

Barley tried to follow the Kind Man farther along the road, but there were too many soldiers walking directly behind the Kind Man as he carried the heavy wood up to the crest of the hill. So Barley turned around and began to walk back through the crowd, burrowing his way through the forest of legs, back to the rocky cliffside where he could climb above the crowd-choked street and then descend to a place farther ahead along the Kind Man's ghastly procession.

Barley descended to the low point of the hill, a spot about a hundred yards ahead of where the Kind Man was walking. Barley watched the Kind Man stagger toward him, moving even slower than he had just minutes before.

Barley looked around at the crowd as he waited for the Kind Man to reach the spot where he stood. At this distance from the spectacle, the people now surrounding Barley were more subdued than the ravenous spectators in the street who pushed for the best view they could get of the suffering man. Many of the people Barley was now standing among seemed appalled at what was being done to the Kind Man. They shook their heads and clasped their hands up to their mouths as they witnessed his horrific plight.

Barley noticed one old woman staring up the street at the Kind Man and crying.

As Barley looked around, he noticed a man with dark skin standing up against a building, away from the crowd. This man's body was lean and strong, and his manner seemed quiet and gentle. Barley saw that the man's forehead was furrowed with sadness as he watched the Kind Man's slow, painful journey along the road.

Some members of the crowd on the fringes of the event seemed as though they were visitors to the city, people who had stumbled upon the scene and were stunned and rattled by the barbaric ritual they saw. Barley noticed two men talking to each other who wore tunics shaped in a way that was new to Barley. They spoke to each other in quiet, sorrowful tones and seemed to be deeply troubled by the events unfolding before them.

An awful gasp erupted suddenly from the crowd around Barley.

Barley turned just in time to see the Kind Man succumbing to the momentum of the steep, downward slope of the road, which caused the top-heavy wood to carry him forward too fast for his legs to keep up.

Once again the Kind Man plummeted down onto the street.

Barley's eyes fell on a group of men in the crowd down below grinning and nudging each other excitedly at the sight of the Kind Man sprawled on the ground. Then Barley's alert eyes moved to the soldier who had beaten the Kind Man the last time he had fallen.

Again, the soldier, whip in hand, strode quickly toward the Kind Man, who was facedown but trying weakly to lift his head off the road.

Barley turned his head away.

Barley looked around at the crowd, many of whom were shoving their way in to get closer to the violent scene, gawking with a curiosity bordering on delight. Barley then turned and looked up at those people nearer to him, the few gentler souls being undone by the sight of the Kind Man's suffering. His eyes returned to the dark-skinned man who was so distressed by what he saw that he pressed the back of his head to the wall and closed his eyes. Though he was a man of rock-hard muscle, he looked as though he were trying not to weep.

Barley turned his eyes back to the Kind Man and saw that the soldier was unfurling his whip and drawing it back as far as his thick arm could stretch.

But before the soldier could once again bring his whip down onto the back of the Kind Man, he was halted by another soldier whose uniform and manner bespoke a higher rank.

Then a group of soldiers, including the soldier with the whip, gathered to confer. They seemed suddenly concerned and spoke in muted voices, until one soldier blurted out loudly, "If he dies here, before we have displayed him on Golgotha as the Prefect ordered, it will be all our necks!"

The crowd had begun to rumble impatiently, and the soldiers looked at each other nervously. They knew they had to get things moving again.

The crowd began to raise its discontent into a storm of

yelling but was suddenly quieted by the booming, author-
itative voice of a soldier who seized the crowd's attention
with one loud word.

"You!"

The soldier lifted his armored forearm and pointed the
index finger of his leather-gloved hand and said it again.

"You!"

"Me?" asked the dark-skinned man.

The large, strong-looking man was an easy target for
the soldier's searching eye.

"Me?" the man asked again.

"Yes, you, stranger."

The soldier summoned him with an emphatic wave.

The man seemed uneasy but walked over to the soldier
and listened attentively as he was given orders. Then Barley
saw the man walk over to the Kind Man where he lay in the
street, trying his best to hoist his wilting body back onto
his feet.

The stranger offered the Kind Man his thick forearm
to hold on to as he tried to pull himself up from the ground.
Slowly, the Kind Man reached up his trembling hand and
clutched tightly to his arm. Then Barley saw the powerful
stranger hoist the full weight of the Kind Man up with ease.
Barley noticed that the Kind Man kept hold of the stranger's
arm with the hand he used to hoist himself up and placed

his other hand on the stranger's same arm, patting it gently three times.

Once the stranger was sure the Kind Man was steady on his feet, he went over to the piece of wood, lifted it with a slight grunt, and laid it across his own right shoulder. Then the stranger flexed his left arm up so the Kind Man could lean on his forearm. In this way, the two men continued to walk through the clamoring crowd.

CHAPTER 14

The mob of citizens had been steadily increasing, and as it did, Barley noticed that the mood of the crowd grew more hostile. The scattered clusters of people who had watched with compassion in their eyes for the Kind Man were now being shouted over and pushed back by men and women who seemed very angry with the Kind Man. Many in the crowd cried out with indignation that the man they'd come to watch was not carrying his own burden but was instead being assisted by a dark-skinned stranger. Some people shouted out in anger at the stranger as well.

Barley watched as the procession approached. The

Kind Man was moving slowly, just behind the stranger, and progressing haltingly, coming closer to where Barley was now standing at the curb.

Barley watched a few more of the Kind Man's labored paces, and then the Kind Man finally passed right in front of Barley. Barley stood still. He was now beginning to understand that the Kind Man was being led to a terrible place and was moving toward it, more and more broken with each step. Barley could see that the Kind Man's eyes stared forward in a daze and that he was unable to raise his feet beyond a shuffle. All Barley could do was watch and follow him.

Once the Kind Man and the stranger had moved farther along the road, Barley turned to see how large the crowd following the procession was. He saw a parade of citizens snaking up through the city as far as the eye could see, pushing forward as the gloom of this sunless afternoon settled over the city.

Barley allowed the stream of humanity to carry him forward, stepping cautiously so as to dodge the shoving and stomping of the increasingly uncivil crowd. Desperately trying to keep pace with the Kind Man, Barley squirmed, darted, pivoted, using all of his agility to move forward alongside him.

Anytime Barley sensed even a momentary break in the crowd's incessant pushing, he would look through the legs of the crowd at the Kind Man as he staggered along the road. Everything the Kind Man had endured was now draining the beautiful light from his eyes. Sometimes Barley would let his gaze linger too long on the Kind Man and come within an inch of being crushed by some tramping citizen.

The mob of citizens waiting in the distance near the city gate was even louder and more uncivilized than those now pushing in from the other direction. A large group of rowdy young men entered the already out-of-hand crowd, hollering with glee as they elbowed their way to leer and cheer at the spectacle. Barley was now in the middle of all these converging hordes.

Barley could see the soldiers beginning to move the stranger away from the Kind Man so he would have to carry the crossbar alone up to the hill of Golgotha. At the sight of this exchange of the wooden crossbeam from the stranger's shoulder onto the bloody back of the condemned, a huge shout went up from the crowd. Many of the men began to shout, "Crucify him! Crucify him!"

Suddenly the crowd was moving less and shouting more, their collective roar aimed at the Kind Man. Barley looked up as the noise of the crowd rose around him, filling his acute ears until they rang and stung. And soon the shouting became even louder, building to a full-throated rhythm that pulsated in unison.

"Cru-ci-fy him!"

"Cru-ci-fy him!"

"Cru-ci-fy him!"

Barley stood amid the throng, still watching. He saw that the stranger had been forced to step away from the Kind Man, the soldiers backing him off the road and back into the crowd. As they did, Barley saw that the stranger never took his eyes off the Kind Man.

And though weighed down once again by the heavy wood, the Kind Man lifted his head and gazed across the road, looking into the stranger's eyes with a gentle look of thankfulness for the man's help.

Barley kept his eyes on the stranger as he stood amid the crowd, watching the Kind Man struggle on his own with the heavy crossbeam. After a moment, the stranger averted his eyes and sat down by the roadside, his head bowed and his hands covering his eyes. As the procession continued on, the stranger remained where he was. Then Barley noticed the old lady he'd seen earlier with tears on her wrinkled face. She went over and stood by the stranger. Barley saw her touch the back of her wizened hand to the man's face, stroking his cheek. At this gesture from one kind stranger to another, the man looked up at her. Tears flowed down his cheeks and he wept softly.

The roaring chant of the crowd grew stronger. Barley

looked up at a man standing next to him and saw that he had his young son, a boy about three years old, sitting on his shoulders. The father began to chant with the rest of the crowd, "Cru-ci-fy him!" Soon the little boy began to pat his father's head to the beat of the chant and to shout along with the masses.

The procession moved along a narrower stretch of road. The dense and unruly crush of citizens swarmed the street, and Barley froze with panic as the enveloping crowd pushed in all around him. Fearing the mob had begun to get too close to the condemned, the soldiers began using lances and whips to hold the advancing people back. Within seconds they had cleared a perimeter around the condemned, though a tidal wave of yelling men still encroached on the space.

Into this newly formed clearing around the Kind Man came a sight that few in this rabid crowd ever could have expected. Barley watched as a small group of women, moving together as one, pushed their way forward.

When people saw what this cluster of women dared to do, the noise of the throng died down for a few moments. The street became fraught with a different kind of tension as many in the crowd gasped at the defiance these women showed in pushing past the soldiers to draw nearer to the Kind Man.

Barley saw how small of frame these women seemed compared to the giant soldiers they had defied to stand where they now stood.

Most of the women were the age of young mothers, and indeed, many had their children with them. Some were holding infants in their arms, others held the hands of toddlers, and a few mothers had older children of seven or eight years, whose small heads they pressed into their waists to shield their impressionable eyes from the ugly scene around them.

It was clear to Barley that these women had something they wished to say to the Kind Man.

But they did not speak.

They could not.

Seeing the Kind Man before them now—so hurt and so weak, yet still radiating a compassion that each of these mothers hoped their children would grow up to feel—words fell short. The only way these brave women of Jerusalem could speak to the Kind Man was with the honest eloquence of tears.

The crowd at large was rebelling vehemently against this show of sentiment. Groups of young men suddenly formed an angry pack. They began to yell hateful words at the weeping women in wild and guttural tones as they elbowed and muscled their way toward them. But two of the soldiers lifted their lances across the chests of this angry mob and strained to hold the young men back.

Barley could see that the Kind Man had been speaking to the women.

He saw the Kind Man look down at the women's children with a look of great compassion. Then, his body wobbling under the weight of the cross, the Kind Man turned around to face the crowd.

At this gesture, the crowd roared and raged themselves into a frenzy.

The group of young men behind Barley pressed against the soldiers' lances to try to get close enough to the condemned man to strike him or spit on him. A few of them pushed with such force that one of the soldier's lances gave way just long enough to allow the young men to launch powerful darts of spit into the air toward the condemned.

Barley looked back toward the Kind Man and saw the immense sorrow in his eyes as he turned away from the crowd. The Kind Man looked back into the faces of the bereaved women with his gentle eyes and drew a breath to try to speak.

Barley stepped forward.

The Kind Man's eyes moved from the weeping women and sadly scanned the faces of all their children. With profound emotion thickening his voice, he said, "If people do these things when the tree is green, what will happen when it is dry?"

Then Barley watched the Kind Man turn from the women to look up at the rest of the crowd. Barley could see him blinking back pain, straining his bleary eyes to take in the faces of the people, absorbing for a last moment the shapes and sizes and sounds of the citizens before turning to trudge the last of his way through the city.

Soon the procession reached the gate through which the condemned were led to the infamous place of death, the hill of Golgotha. Clustered now around that gate was a group of people clearly not from the city. These were poor people, wastrels coming from the path that led to Golgotha, and foreigners. But Barley could see these people loved the Kind Man, because as soon as they laid eyes on him, a wail of emotion overtook them as the soldiers forcefully stopped them from pushing toward the condemned, just as other soldiers were still keeping back the crush of screaming young men with their makeshift barricade of lances.

The road was now clear for the procession to pass through the gate to Golgotha, and Barley had pressed himself up against a curb several feet from the screaming men. It was a spot he intended to remain in to stay safe from the volatile convergence of people surrounding the gate.

But then he heard someone screaming, over and over, in a voice Barley recognized.

"Save him! Please!"

He looked up and saw Prisca in the middle of the crowd just outside the gate, her face soaked with tears, her arms reaching out to the Kind Man. Barley barked as loud as he could to let her know he was there, but the noise of the crowd was too great for his message to reach her. Prisca did not take her eyes from the Kind Man as he passed in front of her. Barley leapt from the safety of the curb he was crouched against and ran toward Prisca just as he heard her call out, in a voice filled with a life of emotion, one word.

"Jesus . . . !"

It was the last thing Barley heard before the crowd of angry men broke through the soldiers' lances, trampling forward, overwhelming him, till everything in Barley's world went dark.

CHAPTER 15

When Barley opened his eyes, his little body was pressed up against the heavy curb of the street.

The world around him was quiet.

Barley slowly lifted himself from the road, rising onto all fours. He stood reorienting himself for a few seconds, then gave his head a quick, ear-flapping shake.

Barley looked into the distance, toward Golgotha.

Golgotha was not a high hill but rather a gray and craggy outcropping of rock with no vegetation or life growing from it. The way up was steep, and the only path was rocky and uneven. The hill was situated so that when approached from its far side by people walking toward the city, new arrivals to Jerusalem were routinely greeted with the silhouettes of crucifixes visible against the sky. These crosses were a totem of the severity of Roman justice and a warning to all visitors who might dare to transgress it.

Barley could see that the tail end of the procession was now wending its way up the sheer path to the flattened hilltop.

Barley proceeded with haste along the road leading to the hill where the Kind Man had been led.

He arrived quickly at the hillside, and when he had climbed halfway up the side of Golgotha, Barley heard another sound.

It was not the sound of human voices.

This noise reverberated off the stony face of Golgotha.

It was the dull crack of iron being struck.

It was hammering.

Barley could hear the loud, leaden thud as he arrived at the small knoll encircling the crest of Golgotha.

Atop the knoll, Barley found himself dangerously close to the line of soldiers keeping stern watch on the clearing below, their backs to Barley. The crown of the hill sloped down to a flat area at the center of the hilltop. All that Barley could see at first was a sea of billowing red capes fluttering off the soldiers' backs as they stood in front of him in the gusting wind. The wind began to blow so fiercely that Barley dug his paws into the dirt to keep from losing his balance and squinted his eyes as the gritty gray dust of Golgotha blew into his face from the clearing below.

After a few moments, the wind died down into silence, and the soldiers' capes fell slack so they no longer obscured Barley's view. Little by little, the murky dust whipped up by the wind began to settle.

What Barley saw then was a sight he never could have imagined.

There before him was the Kind Man, hanging several feet in the air, his arms stretched wide, his hands nailed to the crossbeam he'd been forced to carry through the street, his feet nailed to the upright post that was anchored in the ground. The Kind Man's body hung limply, and his breathing was labored. Next to the Kind Man was a foreign-looking man who had been nailed to another cross. This man winced angrily, in great agony. On the other side of the Kind Man was another cross with a man nailed to it.

It was Samid.

It was Barley's master.

His master, who he had lost, was in front of him. And yet what Barley saw before him was a human being, nailed to a piece of wood, in a place from which Samid had no hope of ever being saved.

Barley stared at his master.

Samid's arms were wrenched wide, his head hanging low, his eyes half closed, his breathing raspy and audible to Barley even from several feet away.

Every instinct inside of Barley compelled him to let his master know that his dog had found him and was here. Barley ran a few feet in front of the soldiers, planted his four legs in Samid's direction, and boldly let out three quick, full-throated, unapologetic barks.

Barley had hardly finished his third bark before he felt himself hoisted up sharply under his haunches, lifted by a soldier's heavy lance and hurled through the air. Barley landed with a thud and slid a few feet before crashing against the side of a large rock.

As the soldier returned to formation and Barley recovered himself, he lifted his snout up over the rock to look at Samid.

Barley hoped his master had heard him bark.

But Barley could see Samid had not moved at all. He was in the exact same position, his breathing still raspy, but now a little slower.

Barley walked a few paces down the knoll to put some distance between himself and the soldiers. He laid his belly on the ground but kept his head up and looked out across the clearing toward his master and the Kind Man.

All Barley could do was watch and wait.

The minutes and hours of his watch hung heavier than the bleak clouds overhead.

Samid's head drooped even further. His eyes remained closed, and his face was strained with pain. He seemed to have no awareness of his surroundings.

And then there was the Kind Man.

As Barley looked at the Kind Man, he noticed that a group of people stood far forward of the soldiers, very near the foot of the cross on which the Kind Man hung.

A younger man was standing there, just a few yards away from the Kind Man. Barley thought this man must be one of the Kind Man's friends.

Barley saw two women standing just a few feet in front of the Kind Man's friend. One woman was younger, the other older. Both of these women seemed worried and very sad, but they held their heads high as they gazed into the face of the Kind Man.

Barley saw a third woman. She stood closest to the Kind Man, just a few feet from the foot of his cross.

This woman's back was to Barley, and she was standing very still, looking up at the Kind Man, her head tilted at an angle that touched Barley, even seeing it from behind.

And the robe she wore also absorbed Barley's attention. It was blue.

Not a bright blue, but a blue that seemed vivid and

beautiful, a blue that reminded Barley of the color of the wooden bird Duv had made that had come to life and winked at Barley.

Barley knew that the lady in blue was the Kind Man's mother.

He could tell by the way she looked up at her son.

Barley could also tell she was his mother by the way the Kind Man looked back at the lady. He looked at her as though she was the last person in the world he could bear to see hurt. Whenever the Kind Man's eyes met his mother's, Barley saw that he would work to ease the pain on his face, to protect her from seeing his agony. Barley could also see her eyes trying to tell the Kind Man not to worry about her, that she wanted to be there, by her son, at his feet.

Barley lay down and resumed his watch of his master and of the Kind Man and his mother. After a long while, Barley's eyes began to drift up at the sky overhead. The clouds were shifting and swarming and making restless movements and ugly shapes over Golgotha.

Suddenly, Barley was startled by a sharp cry.

"You . . . !"

The terrible voice cracked through the silence in a way that made even the soldiers look up with a start.

The voice belonged to the dark-featured man who was hanging on the cross on the other side of the Kind Man.

The man had turned his head and was looking angrily

at the Kind Man. His face was weary with pain, but his eyes were fiery with bitterness and rage.

"You . . ."

Then the man's voice softened to a rasp. He drew a huge breath and spoke with such a seething roar that his voice echoed over the hill.

"If you be the Christ . . ."

There was silence as the agitated man tried to draw another large breath. By now, most of the people who were watching from the knoll—especially the soldiers—had their eyes fixed on this raving man.

But Barley's eyes were pulled elsewhere.

He saw that Samid had lifted his head.

Barley got up off the ground to all fours—paws poised, ears lifted, every muscle in his body alert.

Samid was very weak, but Barley could see that he was awake and aware enough to turn his head in the direction that the startling voice had come from.

Barley and Samid listened along with the crowd as the prisoner spoke to the Kind Man, trying to finish the scornful sentence he had begun several gasps before.

"Aren't you the Messiah?"—his voice now fuller, stronger—"save yourself and us!"

The man's plea resounded through the dusky sky before trailing into silence.

Then Samid spoke.

He leaned his head forward with difficulty and looked over at the man who had just spoken.

Samid said to the man sadly, "Don't you fear God?"

Then Samid's voice grew stronger as he slowly continued. "We are punished justly, for we are getting what our deeds deserve."

Samid rolled his head back against the wood of his cross to better look into the face of the Kind Man on the cross next to him.

Samid continued, "But this man has done nothing wrong."

Then Samid's chin began to shake, and his whole being collapsed into weeping. He spoke no words as the tears coursed down his bedraggled cheeks. Barley saw in Samid's eyes the same look he remembered when his master's strength and voice had cracked, in words once spoken to Prisca.

"I've done bad things in life, been mean and drunk and stole . . ."

Now Barley watched as his master's hardness broke away and the tears of a lifetime poured forth.

As Samid wept, Barley saw the Kind Man turn and look at Samid with compassion.

Then Barley saw Samid lift his weeping head and look directly into the eyes of the Kind Man.

"Lord?" Samid called softly to the Kind Man.

The Kind Man looked deep into Samid's eyes as Samid paused to gather his strength.

"Jesus . . . remember me when you come into your kingdom."

The Kind Man gave Samid a look of such radiant kindness that Barley was transfixed. Then Barley heard the Kind Man speak to his master.

"Truly I tell you, today you will be with me in paradise."

At these words, Barley saw his master's pained face begin to ease and then brighten ever so faintly into a droopy grin, just enough for Barley to see a bit of Samid's broken teeth.

Samid had changed. And Barley saw it.

Now Samid lowered his head and his breathing became calmer. He sank into a quiet unconsciousness, his eyes half closed as he continued to breathe more peacefully.

But Barley still needed to let his master know that he was there.

As the minutes hung heavily, Barley kept alert. He would wait.

He would know the right moment to let his master know his dog was there.

Soon Barley began to notice that the clouds were getting darker and lower. Everything was quiet and still and gray and cold.

All three men were now breathing very slowly, and all three of their heads were lowered.

Then, a sudden motion.

It was the Kind Man.

He lifted his head—not weakly, but with a quick burst of waning strength. Barley watched intently as the Kind Man looked around, moving his head very slowly. The Kind Man did not look at his friends or his mother. Instead, he looked at the soldiers, some of whom were keeping watch, some sitting at leisure after having done their duty of nailing men to crosses. Another small group of soldiers sat off to the side, playing dice to alleviate the boredom of this routine deathwatch, and one or two were actually looking up at the Kind Man with, if not sadness, then a touch of shame.

After looking at all of these people for several moments, the Kind Man lifted his eyes upward toward the cloud-filled sky and spoke.

"Father, forgive them, for they do not know what they are doing."

The Kind Man lowered his head once again, breathing softly, then looked up into the sky and spoke in a loud and anguished voice.

"My God, my God, why have you forsaken me?"

The agony of the Kind Man's words reached Barley's

sensitive ears, and Barley sensed that the clouds themselves were hearing and feeling this man's agony.

Barley's eyes moved instinctually toward the Kind Man's mother. He saw that she was standing at the foot of the Kind Man's cross, still and graceful. She neither turned away nor winced but looked at her son and let her eyes tell him all he needed to know.

Barley realized the lady in blue was now being separated from her son. He turned to look up at the Kind Man, who was very still. Barley understood what this meant.

The Kind Man had died.

CHAPTER 16

Within moments, a terrible, slow rumbling began. At first it was a low, rolling hum that grew rapidly. Soon it felt to Barley as though some deep abyss inside the hill was going to open up and cry out at all it had witnessed.

Barley dug his paws into the earth to try to steady himself as he looked up into the sky. The clouds raced overhead, buffeted by strong gusts of moaning wind. Soon their sodden shapes began to billow down and out, filling the low sky above the Kind Man's cross, and a deluge began to pummel Golgotha with a gray torrent.

Barley stood, gazing at his master through the rain.

Samid's chest moved slowly up and down as he struggled to draw breath, his eyes half open and dazed, his lips pursed with pain. Barley remained there, unfazed by the heavy downpour that soon drenched his scraggily white fur until his pink skin showed through. Barley blinked repeatedly to keep the pelting drops from obscuring his view of his master.

As Barley peered through the blinding rain, he could see Samid's body coming to the end of its long struggle.

But Barley still needed his master to know that he was there and to understand that he had found him and would stay by him to the last.

Time was running out.

Barley looked around and noticed that a number of soldiers were milling about anxiously. He could tell that some new concern had all the men on edge. The soldiers were looking up and pointing at the Kind Man, whose deceased body remained on the cross. It was now late in the day on Friday, and tomorrow was the Sabbath. The Sabbath was the one day of the week that those crucified on Golgotha could not be left hanging on their crosses as a warning. Such a display during Sabbath would be deemed an abomination. The bodies of the condemned must be removed by sundown on Friday.

Barley could tell by the way the soldiers were now looking and pointing that they were no longer discussing the Kind Man. They were concerning themselves with the man hanging on the cross on the other side of the Kind Man. This angry wretch was still groaning loudly and his breathing was not nearly as weak as Samid's. Soon a few more soldiers came over to stand below that man's cross and join in the discussion.

After a short time, two of the soldiers left the group and moved hastily in Barley's direction as they walked across the center of the clearing to the foot of Samid's cross.

As the soldiers approached, Barley huddled his head down into his shoulders, hoping to escape their notice. But Barley heard a fierce slicing sound and looked up just in time to step away from the snap of a whip lashing down onto the muddy ground next to him, missing him by inches and sending a spray of mud several feet into the air.

Then the soldier reared back the whip again, this time with double the gusto. Driven by a mix of instinct and will, Barley launched into a full gallop, with flying swirls of mud trailing behind. He charged through the downpour until he was well out of range of the soldier and his whip.

Barley now stood several yards from the crosses and watched.

The whip-wielding soldier and his superior walked over to look at the man who was writhing and moaning on the cross on the other side of the Kind Man. Then they walked over and looked up at Samid. The men could see that Samid was still breathing, his chest rising and falling in a strong, steady rhythm. Barley watched as the men shook their heads in dismay. Then they turned away and walked to the middle of the clearing to join the other soldiers. The men began to argue with each other so heatedly that Barley could hear their angry voices even through the driving wind and rain.

The commanding soldier turned and hollered through the rain to a younger—and very muscular—soldier who was standing off to the side near Barley. His words were emphatic.

"We need to finish this!"

The burly younger soldier heard this and gestured respectfully to the commander. This man was huge but baby-faced, an up-and-coming underling, the sort of soldier known in the ranks to be eager, able, and deadly. Barley saw that he was carrying a long, heavy pole that seemed to be made of iron. The soldier walked over to the cross that held the raging man, who was, by now, more subdued—his eyes wandering dazedly, his exhales sounding like low moans.

The commander gave the soldier a businesslike nod. Barley watched as the soldier cocked back the heavy iron bar and, with one brutal stroke, swung it forward, smashing the prisoner's legs with a deafening crack as the man's weakened body collapsed, hanging from his nailed hands, swaying back and forth for a few terrible moments to the rhythmic creaking of the wooden crossbar strained by the dead man's weight, until all motion ebbed to stillness.

Barley stared up at the man sadly for a moment, until he saw the soldier with the iron bar walking toward Samid.

Barley ran down from the knoll, charging through the mud toward Samid's cross as the soldier planted his booted feet in the ground and tightened his grip on the iron bar. Barley kept running even as he recoiled when he saw the blow his master took.

The sound of the bar landing seemed to shake the whole hill, but Samid did not utter a sound as he crumpled down, his chest still heaving with breath. Their brutal business done and certain the nameless thief on the cross was now breathing his last, the soldiers walked away.

Barley reached the foot of Samid's cross just as the soldiers slowly sauntered away.

Barley remained.

And then he began to bark.

He barked full and loud and strong. But Samid did not move. So Barley barked and barked again.

Barley barked, but Samid gave no reaction.

There was only silence. And not so much as the tiniest response from Samid.

Barley tried again.

Barley barked to tell not only his master but to tell every cruel soldier on the whole evil ground of Golgotha who Barley belonged to.

But again, no reaction from Samid.

Now Barley stood there.

Looking up.

Silent.

Waiting for any sign his master had heard him.

Barley blinked a few times, not shifting his eyes from his watchful focus on his motionless master. Samid's breath was so slow now that Barley had to strain to discern whether his master still breathed at all.

Barley blinked and waited.

Then Samid began to lift his head.

Slowly . . . slowly . . .

His anguished eyes were dazed. His mouth hung open, his cheeks quivering in pain. The soldiers watched as suddenly Samid opened his eyes very wide, something the soldiers knew was often a sign of the final moments of life.

When Samid's eyes opened, they fell directly upon Barley.

Barley knew his master was looking down at him and was certain he could see what he wanted his master to know.

That his dog was there.

Then Barley saw it.

The lifted jaw, his master's lips parting ever so slightly. And finally, the broken tooth.

His master had tried to smile at him.

Then Samid slowly closed his eyes and died.

CHAPTER 17

Barley stood in the rain—a small, sodden figure on the hill of Golgotha. The moment Samid died, Barley had turned his head away. He could feel that his master was gone, but Barley could not bring himself to leave.

Barley's eyes were drawn to the activity at the Kind Man's cross.

A ladder had been placed up against it, and soldiers were preparing to remove the body. The men used iron tongs to pull off the strange circle of barbs that Barley had seen around the Kind Man's head, and the now-unfurled braid of thorns was tossed onto the muddy ground just a few feet away from Barley.

Then came the nails.

The first one slammed onto the ground near the thorns with such force that a splash of mud flew high in the air.

They were as thick around as a man's finger, but twice as long, each with a gnarled point that made the hurtful thorns seem gentle. The soldiers were using a thick, flat metal tool to pry them from the Kind Man's hands and feet, grunting till they tossed the freed nail down onto the accumulating junk pile of their day's bloody work.

Barley had watched the first nail land.

Then the second.

Then the third and longest nail, warped by having been pounded through the Kind Man's coupled feet, landed almost upright in the mud.

The group of people who had stayed with the lady in blue were gathered near the base of the Kind Man's cross. There was an older man standing among them whom Barley hadn't noticed before. He was mostly bald with light gray hair on the sides and wore brightly colored clothes made of rich fabrics. Barley knew he must be important by the way the soldiers spoke to him—less gruffly and rudely than they spoke to everyone else, even to each other.

This man had been speaking to the commanding soldier, who had called an order up to the soldiers on the ladder and then walked away. Once that head soldier was gone, the well-dressed old man began to reverently unfurl a length of clean white cloth with the help of a lady with long hair and a younger man who had been standing next to him.

The older man, the young-faced man, and the lady were now holding the outstretched cloth under the cross. The soldiers on the ladder had taken hold of the Kind Man's body and were lowering it down to the group waiting below. But one of the soldiers lost his grip on the Kind Man's rain-slicked skin, and the body fell awkwardly, dangling unevenly until the Kind Man's friends were able to maneuver it to the center of the cloth. The small group of followers paused for a moment, standing very still, holding the body of the Kind Man.

Then the lady in blue walked over and stood beside her son.

The Kind Man's head was thrown back, hanging limply. Barley could see that the part of a man's throat that moves up and down when he laughs was jutting out sharply. And the Kind Man's hair was draped across his bloody face.

The Kind Man's mother gently placed her right hand under her son's head and slowly raised it up, allowing it to rest against her body. Then she reached over with her other hand and used one of her fingers to move aside the veil of hair covering the Kind Man's face.

Barley could see that, even now, his face looked kind.

After a few quiet moments, the older man touched her shoulder. The soldiers were becoming impatient. The Kind Man's mother nodded knowingly. Then she turned back and stared down one last time into the face of her son.

Barley saw a look in her eyes that he had seen before.

It was the look of a mother who has to let her son go.

After a long moment the Kind Man's mother closed her eyes, turned her head away, and stepped back from her son's body. The Kind Man's friends wrapped his body in the white cloth, and soon the older gentleman nodded to the group, indicating it was time to go.

Barley could see the deep pain etched on the younger man's face and understood that he felt lost without his master but was trying to be brave. The young man's strength was needed to bear most of the Kind Man's weight, and then the old man joined him, gently hoisting the body into a carrying position.

As they moved, one of the Kind Man's lower limbs slipped from under the cloth. The young man stopped and turned his head away at the ugly sight of the wound. But Barley saw the woman with the long hair calmly walk over, gently take hold of the Kind Man's foot, and press it to her face sweetly—like it was not ugly at all—before placing it back under the cloth. Barley understood this. The foot of the master is always beautiful—there to walk beside you, the familiar flap of his sandal tapping reassuring music as he leads you on the way. On days when Duv was at the market and Barley missed him, he would sometimes curl up next to one of Duv's old sandals to feel better. Barley hoped the Kind Man's friends had an old sandal of his to keep nearby when they missed him.

As the rain began to fall again, the sparse band of the Kind Man's loved ones made their wobbly way down the hill. As the Kind Man was carried along, Barley watched the white cloth that held him move against the darkened vista surrounding Golgotha, like one bright cloud floating through a troubled sky.

It was a long time—several minutes—before Barley could bring himself to turn his head back around and look at the cross on which Samid's body had been hanging.

It was empty.

Barley felt relieved.

As he stood alone in the rain, he was glad to know his master was somewhere else. He hoped it was a place that had no rain, a place where masters and their dogs could stay together.

CHAPTER 18

Barley looked around and found himself completely alone on Golgotha.

He finally stood up slowly and began the journey down the hill.

Barley was too tired to be hungry and too hungry to be tired. The rain had subsided slightly and had left behind a night sky filled with softly mournful clouds.

Now Barley would do what the only instinct that hadn't yet been shattered by this day told him to.

He would walk. Walk and walk. Walk somewhere, nowhere, anywhere.

By the time the rain had stopped completely, Barley had walked for hours and hours and had traveled for miles.

Darkness had come long ago, and in spite of his exhaustion, Barley kept on moving.

In this way, Barley traveled for much of the night.

At long last he came to a small indentation at the bottom of a low cliff. The mouth of this rocky burrow was positioned so that when Barley crawled into it, he could still see up and down the road. The tiny den was nestled under a large cliff wall, and Barley thought it as fine a home for the night as he was likely to find.

Barley curled himself up puppy-tight to sleep for what he hoped would be an eternity.

And soon Barley's exhausted, rhythmic breathing lulled him into a sleep so deep that not even dreams could reach it.

And he slept.

And slept, and slept.

The weather the next day was neither sunny nor rainy, with dull, pale silver skies that were nice to sleep under. And that was exactly what Barley did.

But this time, he did dream.

Or at least that was how it seemed.

Barley had been having a dream about one of Duv's wooden birds. The figurine had come to life and was flying around Adah and Duv's little house, making a sad sound. It wasn't a singing or chirping but more like crying or a mournful groaning. It was a sound that made Barley feel bad for the little bird.

As Barley lay there in his little den in half-sleep, he suddenly realized he was not dreaming. But he could still hear the bird—faint, but very near.

Then, to Barley's distress, he realized where the sound was coming from. The sound was coming from inside of him. It was the growling of his own stomach—which Barley understood was now so empty there was room enough inside it for a sad bird to be flying around.

Barley had found a fine shelter for himself. But now he knew that if he didn't find some food soon, he would not survive. He had to find either food or a person who would be kind enough to feed him.

Barley crawled out of the snug shelter, sneezed a few times as the sun hit his face, shook his head to rouse his instincts out of their many hours of sleep, and resolved to set out on the hunt for some food. He took a look up and down the road. He saw nothing but rocks and sand and sparse trees that had died long ago. There was not a living man, beast, or flower in sight.

Barley knew he would have to leave his temporary little home in order to find food. He gave one last look back at the small cave and began to trot down the road.

Soon, in spite of his hunger, Barley realized how fine it felt to once again be running with the sun on his back, the wind on his fur.

He made his way over narrow roads and hilly terrain.

After many hours, he found himself on a road that seemed to have no other roads jutting off of it for him to turn down. Barley began to worry. He could tell by the slant of light on the road that the sun would be setting soon. And being caught on a wrong road at night would be dangerous. Hunger would take days to kill him, but a nocturnal desert predator could do the job in seconds.

Just as these worries were swarming in Barley's head, he saw, at the end of this long road, a huge boulder and a small patch of tall grass where the road forked in two different directions.

To the left, the road veered down. To the right, it veered up.

The sun fell across the boulder in a way that made it look warm, so Barley trotted up to the huge rock and stopped in front of it, glancing down one possible direction and up the other. He knew he would have to make a choice. And this would not be easy for Barley. He missed having a master to guide his way and worried what would happen if he chose poorly.

As Barley stood there wondering, he heard the tiniest, faintest sound coming from the grass in front of the big boulder. It was just a soft flutter, but on a quiet road, it reached Barley's ears and made his eyes go wide.

On the end of a blade of grass, just an inch from his nose, Barley saw a butterfly.

He took a step closer, drawn by the butterfly's bold colors and funny flutters. And the butterfly did not seem to mind having a dog look at it so closely. Barley stood for a long while staring at the wings, admiring their perfect patterns and colors. The butterfly reminded Barley of the birds Duv created with the pretty paints Adah made. The butterfly was the first beautiful thing Barley had seen in a long while. After yesterday's dark hours of clouds, rain, muddy iron, blood-soaked wood, and the gray haze of human cruelty over every inch of stony hilltop, the lovely butterfly was a welcome sight indeed.

As Barley observed the butterfly, its delicate wings began flitting more swiftly. Barley wagged his tail as he watched the little creature gracefully rise off the blade of grass then turn and trace ribbons into the air as it flew away and disappeared . . . up the road to the right.

Barley's mind was made up.

If the road to the right was good enough for a butterfly with such nice wings, it was good enough for Barley.

B arley had galloped up the road only a few hundred yards when he saw, on either side of the narrow roadway, off in the distance, some scattered clusters of humble-looking houses. These were smaller even than Adah and Duv's house, but they looked well kept. And most importantly, Barley could smell dinners cooking. He began to step livelier as he continued up the road, hopeful he might find someone who would be kind to him.

But then he saw something strange coming down the hill.

It was a tall, thin, shadowy presence, outlined by the flat light of the late afternoon sky. The figure was clearly that of an old person—twisted, hunched over, and moving with an eerie gait.

As the figure neared, Barley could see it was a man, the cowl of his gray robe thrown over his head in a way that made the man's head look monstrous against the dusky sky. Barley could discern from amid the shadows under the man's cowl a bald head and the mottled skin of a hideous-looking face. Barley could hear the man voicing a mournful, rhythmic, rasping chant.

And this hunched, hooded, disfigured, mumbling figure held a big, heavy stick, gripping it tightly in his hand.

Then Barley heard another sound behind him. As he turned away from the ghoulish, hooded figure, he saw a younger man with reddish hair and a bushy beard ambling up the road from behind. The man was so tall and so broad that to Barley he looked like a giant. He wore a grubby tunic and was making long, fast strides.

With a scary old man coming down at him from one

direction and a redheaded giant coming up at him from the other direction, Barley wondered what sort of place the butterfly had pointed him to.

Barley caught the giant red-headed man's eye as he passed, but the man just looked back at Barley blankly. He was not like most people, who when they see a dog at least say hello or sometimes even stop for a quick pet before passing by. Barley gave the man a good, strong tail wag as he passed by, but the huge man just looked at Barley as though he were invisible and picked up his speed a little as he headed up the road toward the scary man.

Barley watched as the two odd men neared each other.

When they finally met on the road, Barley saw the scary-looking hooded man do an unexpected thing.

He stopped mumbling, bowed politely, and said something through his cowl in a gravelly voice that sounded surprisingly cheery for a scary man with a stick.

Then Barley saw something else he didn't expect.

The redheaded giant lunged at the scary man, clutching the man's cowl with one hand as the other hand held a gleaming blade across the man's throat.

"No! Oh please! Do not—! For your own sake, do not—" The scary man's gravel-voice became loud with fear. But Barley also heard a sweetness in the old man's tone.

"I have so little to take . . ."

Barley realized that this was not a scary man; this was just a poor man, like the people at the camp—who weren't scary, just poor.

Barley watched as the giant robber put out his wide leg and yanked his victim's cloak until the poor man tripped, sending his stick flying into the air and his tall, hunched frame toppling onto the road so hard that Barley could feel the street shake under his paws.

Barley did not know what to do.

Then the robber pointed his knife down toward the poor man's face.

"You need not use that. Please . . ." the poor man rasped as the robber began to pat the poor man's body forcefully, looking for his coin purse.

Barley saw the poor man trying to rise onto his knees, reaching into the pocket of his tunic for his money. He said gently to the robber, "I shall give you what you wish, friend!"

To which the red-haired man growled, "I am not your friend!" and kicked dirt in the man's face. But the poor man looked up at his attacker and said kindly, "You need not use a knife. You may take all I have."

And he reached up and handed the robber, not a proper coin purse, but a small, tied rag.

The robber tore it open and saw what was in it.

Just two small coins.

"That's all?" the man bellowed, furious.

The robber was enraged he had gone to so much trouble for so few coins. He stormed a few paces away from the man, reached down to the ground, and picked up the poor man's heavy walking stick. Then he walked back to the poor man, stood over him, and gripped the stick in his beefy hands as he raised it up over the man's frail chest.

When he saw this, Barley felt anger rise in him.

He had seen so much evil over the last day.

Now he would finally strike back at it.

Barley ran up the road toward the two men.

Once he got to the giant redheaded man, he would bite!

But just as Barley reached the two men, he heard a familiar sound.

"Give us today our daily bread . . ."

The robber was standing over the poor man who was kneeling in the street, his bald head bowed and his raspy voice calmly reciting the same sweet and solemn words that he had been mumbling to himself when he was first limping down the road.

"And forgive us our debts, as we also have forgiven our debtors."

These were words Barley had heard before, and they were spoken in the same soft murmur Barley had heard over almost eight years of life with Adah and Duv.

Barley understood.

The poor man was a follower of the Kind Man.

He also understood that, with these words in his ears, he would not be able to bite the redheaded giant.

The only problem was, Barley was still racing at top speed up the road in attack mode. And he had no plan.

Barley wished at this moment he had a master to give him some guidance, but he didn't have a master to guide him.

Or did he?

That's when it dawned on Barley what he should do.

He had learned it from Adah and Duv, as he saw them live humbly and treat each other sweetly in a house filled with simple joys. And finally from Samid, who was strong enough, even at the last, to look at his dog and try to smile. And these masters had all learned it from their master—the Kind Man, whom Barley had seen look with boundless love at a weeping thief on a cross and see only a lost child whom he asked to follow him home.

B arley now understood the lesson of lessons—the way to overcome evil.

Look for the good.

Look for the good, and forgive.

Running like a champion, Barley announced his arrival

on the scene by launching himself through the air—arcing over the fallen body of the thin, bald man and right into the unsuspecting arms of the redheaded robber.

The stunned man looked down, amazed at how fast he'd gone from robbing a man with a knife to holding a scruffy white dog in his arms. Having dropped his knife and the poor man's walking stick instinctively to catch the foreign body flying toward him, the robber was now defenseless.

Before the robber could react, Barley began to lick his bearded face wildly. He was looking for the good! The giant didn't know what to do. He just stood there confused, frustrated, and embarrassed that a thief of his size and experience was making such a poor job of robbing.

The man heaved Barley out of his arms and into the air. Barley landed hard in a sprawl, but he shook himself up to all fours quickly and ran back toward the giant.

The robber bent his wide frame down and picked up his knife. Then he planted his feet firmly as Barley sped toward him, his knife pointed forward and at the ready.

Barley raced toward the robber with all his might and launched himself into the air with the force of a small and well-aimed projectile. As Barley slammed headfirst into the giant's legs, the robber let out a scream that was almost as high as the arc the knife made flying out of his hand. It landed with a clank on the street between the robber and

Barley. Dazed as Barley was from the collision, he collected himself and ran immediately for the knife, while the giant scrambled on all fours to reach the knife first.

Barley won.

Now Barley held the handle of the knife in his snout like a fetching stick and began running around the robber in speedy circles.

The giant roared, now purple with rage.

"Give me that, you lunatic cur!"

As the robber lurched down to grab the knife from Barley, Barley pivoted and ran in the other direction. And when the robber tried to grab the knife again, Barley repeated this tactic. Barley and the giant engaged in this silly dance for so long that the robber got dizzy and had to stop for a moment. But Barley drew him back to the game through one of the oldest tricks known to dogs. He trotted up and dropped the knife just inches in front of the man's feet. When the man doubled over to grasp it, Barley scooped it up before he even had a chance and started a new round of his crazy game as the robber chased, panted, and swore.

It was at this point that Barley and the robber began to hear loud, feisty laughter.

They heard the raspy, gravelly chuckling of the poor man who—still on the ground and with dirt on his face— was watching all of this and loudly cackling at the heroic little dog who had arrived on the scene and was giving the giant robber quite a time of it.

The exhausted redheaded man was growing tired of Barley's game and moved to end the humiliating escapade by returning his focus to what he had come for—the poor man's coins.

"To blazes with a knife," he said to himself. "I'll beat his pathetic money out of him!"

He ran toward the old man.

But so did Barley.

And Barley got there sooner. By the time the robber reached the old man, Barley had deposited the knife into the old man's lap, who now held it up at the robber. The giant man found himself in the awkward position of being a defenseless robber facing a knife-wielding victim and tail-wagging dog.

The robber at long last admitted defeat and turned to flee.

"Here, sir," the old man said. "I believe this belongs to you."

The robber turned around to see the poor man holding the knife out toward him. Sensing some kind of trick, the robber inched forward slowly, then snatched the knife from his hand in a millisecond and turned on his heels again.

"And here," the poor man said. "I believe you wanted these as well."

The robber turned toward the poor man again to see him holding out his meager couple of coins.

"You must be crazy, old man."

"It's all right," the man said, still holding out the coins. "You may have them."

After hesitating a moment, the robber walked over to the old man and reached for the coins. The robber gasped at seeing the pebbly flesh covering the old man's arms, and when the robber raised his head, he was close enough to see the man's face under his cowl.

The robber screamed as he dropped the coins and backed away.

"The disease! You have the disease!"

The poor man said calmly, "You needn't be afraid. I was afflicted years before."

The robber stared wide-eyed and panicked at the old man. He clutched the knife hard, pushing the point aggressively into the air between them.

After a moment, the poor man tossed the coins at the redheaded man's feet.

"I don't understand," said the robber. "Why would you give these to me?"

"Because I learned to."

"You learned to?"

"From my Teacher." Then the poor man's already broken voice cracked further with deep sadness. "My Teacher who yesterday was crucified by the Romans."

"What teacher, you crazy fool?"

"A man I was brought to see . . . to be healed of this disease."

Then the redheaded man said scornfully, "By the looks of you, he didn't do a very good job of it!"

The poor man lowered his head for a moment.

"Ah . . . yes. They say this is the disease of the poor and the filthy. But I was neither when I became afflicted. I had money, servants, lands, all a man could wish for, until I was struck with this disease. Then I was shunned. I lost all I had. Then . . . I was brought by my family to the Teacher to be healed. But when I listened to what the Teacher said, I realized I had been a prideful, greedy, wicked man. I was callous, cared for nothing but money and property, and was cruel to many, including my own family. The Teacher has said, 'Blessed are the meek, for they will inherit the earth.' He made me see that I was better off and a better man without all that I once had. Hearing his words, I knew that I was already healed."

Then the man smiled sadly.

"But now they have killed my Teacher. Since first I heard

the terrible news last evening from some of his followers, I've walked the streets in prayer."

There was silence.

The robber stared at the man intently. Then he took a step toward Barley and the old man, jutting the knife forward as he inched closer to them. As Barley watched, the poor man placed his hand gently on Barley's back, petting down the soft bristle of his fur that stood on end with fear.

The robber looked at the old man and Barley. Then he looked back at the coins that the old man had thrown at his feet. Then he paused.

The robber stuck the knife into the ground. He looked at the old man and said meekly, "I am sorry."

To which the poor man, rasping through a smile, said, "I forgive you."

The robber turned and, with his head hanging down, walked past the coins without even glancing at them. Barley and the old man watched as the redheaded giant ambled slowly up the road toward the crest of the hill.

CHAPTER 19

After the departure of the robber, Barley and the old man sat together for a time, just resting and enjoying the safety of one another's company. After a time, Barley heard the voice of an approaching man, deep and clear and strong but filled with emotion.

"There you are! Oh! Thank God! Thank God!"

A man ran to the injured old man and buried him in his arms as the old man grasped this younger man closely around his neck and clung to him. This was the first real happiness that Barley had witnessed in days, and it made Barley wag his tail.

"I was so scared when you were gone," the younger man said, near tears. "Our whole neighborhood has been looking for you. We've all been so very worried."

"I am sorry to have worried you. But . . . you heard about the Teacher?"

The old man's raspy voice continued mournfully, "They . . . they . . . cru—" The man's gravelly words trailed off into silent emotion as tears streamed down his scarred cheeks.

The young man hugged him and said, "I know. I know. And I am so sorry for you. And for him. And for us all. For the whole world."

"We mustn't be sorry," the old man said gently, recovering his voice and lifting up his hooded head. "We must love. And care for those who need us. Just as he taught."

The young man released the old man from his tight grasp, looked into his face, and smiled.

"Yes," he replied.

But then the young man gasped sharply when he saw the old man's injured face beneath his cowl.

"You're bleeding," boomed the man's voice in alarm. And he lowered the hurt man's cowl to have a closer look. Barley could now see the man's bald head was covered in what looked like many little rocks made out of flesh.

"I am fine. It's just a scratch," the old man said, lifting

back his cowl and laughing. "And it's the least of my physical defects, wouldn't you say?"

"What happened to you?"

"A huge redheaded man tried to rob me."

"Who? Where is he?" the young man asked, looking around protectively. His eyes suddenly fell, in amazement, on the knife sticking up from the dirt road.

The old man said proudly, "Not to worry, my boy. There is one less robber in this world!"

Staring at the knife, the man's deep voice rose. "You killed him?"

"No, I didn't kill him. I forgave him. It seemed to do the trick." And the old man chuckled.

Then the old man looked at Barley, who stood nearby wagging his tail.

"And I had some help from my little friend here, who saved me!"

The old man patted his thigh and called out to Barley, his raspy voice now full of merriment.

"Come here, little one!"

Barley did not need to be asked twice.

He bolted over to the man and reached up to lick his bumpy face, pushing his snout up into the man's cowl.

The old man said proudly, "This little creature saved your father's life!"

And with that, the other man reached over and began petting Barley vigorously.

"He did? Well, what a good fellow!"

The son was the sort of young buck who knows how to have fun with a dog, and soon he was crouched on all fours, bobbing his head at Barley and swiping his strong arms out at him playfully.

The father watched Barley rise up on his hind legs to bat his front paws at his new playmate.

"Are you my friend?" the young man squealed.

"He likes you, son!"

And then in a special, high-pitched, gritted-teeth voice, through scrunched lips, he squeaked again, "Are you my friend?"

Barley froze.

Time may change a man's face and age and height and weight and hair, but his dog voice never changes. Nor does his dog's reaction to it.

The young man stared intently at Barley's face, examining his eyes, his ears, and especially his snout.

"What is it?" the father asked. "What's wrong, Micah?"

There was silence and stillness for a few long seconds as he continued to stare at Barley's white scruff and runty body and tail set madly wagging by the voice he'd heard.

Then Micah said breathlessly, "This dog . . . he . . . he . . . looks like a pup I had when I was a little boy."

"Oh . . . no . . . you must be mistaken, son," the older man gently corrected him. "Back then I was not the kind of father who would have let you keep a little dog."

"You didn't." Micah looked away.

Then, lowering his eyes, the old man stared at Barley and had a vague memory of something terrible he had done long ago.

"Son . . . it couldn't possibly be that pup."

So Micah tried again.

As he leaned forward on all fours, Barley could see past the square-jawed face that had made the indelible sound to the boyish bright green eyes beyond.

"Are you my friend? Are you *mine*?"

The second Barley heard Micah's dog voice, he dove forward with such zeal he knocked Micah onto his back. Then Barley pranced on his chest, giving him eight years' worth of missed hellos. Micah tried to lift Barley off of him but was laughing so hard he could hardly breathe. He was, however, able to peer up close at Barley's fig of a nose and see the pink splotch his ten-year-old finger had loved to trace.

"Father!" Micah called out after catching his breath. "Father, this *is* the dog I had when I was a boy."

"Oh, Micah! Let me see him," the father pleaded, peeling back the hood of the heavy cowl he kept draped over his forehead, exposing his scarred face, disfigured with the reminders of his disease.

The old man took Barley gently into his arms.

"Oh . . ." he said, his raspy voice thickening with feeling. Then he lowered his face down to Barley's head, closed his eyes, pressed his scarred lips against Barley's fur, and whispered so softly not even Micah could hear what his father was saying.

As Barley leaned against Micah's father, he remained still, held by the same man who long ago had separated him from his mother and from the boy he had loved. And from deep inside this very man, Barley began to hear the same soothing tune he recognized from his mother—*bum-BUM, bum-BUM, bum-BUM.*

In that moment, as the sun was going down on an empty stretch of dirt road, Barley not only forgave the man who took his mother from him, he craned back his small head, looked up into the man's craggy face, and licked him.

"Well," Micah said as he watched, "looks like someone's found a friend."

The old man sat in the road, accepting kisses on a face that had not been kissed in years.

"Micah," he sighed as he held Barley, "our Teacher said,

'It would be better for them to be thrown into the sea with a millstone tied around their neck than to cause one of these little ones to stumble.'"

Micah looked with amusement down at Barley licking his father and said, "Well, he sure doesn't seem too harmed to me!" And he laughed loudly.

"He is not the only little one I'm thinking of."

Micah stopped laughing.

Father and son looked at each other.

"I had in mind a young boy," his father said sadly, "and all the chances for a young son's joy I put a stop to."

Micah smiled understandingly.

"Father, you said that we must now do two things. We must love, and we must care for those who need us. Since this dog has done the first for us, can we do the second for him?"

"Micah," he said decisively as he patted Barley's head, "one thing I will tell you for certain—this dog will live out his days in the home of two followers of the Teacher from Galilee."

Then he gave Barley a little nudge and said, "Go see your master."

Barley walked to Micah's feet and stood looking up at him. As the old man rather spryly attempted to stand up, Micah reached down to help his father and with one strong

RON MARASCO

hoist lifted his frail form up from the ground. Micah made sure his father was steady on his feet, patted his shoulder, and said, "Let's go home."

Then he turned to Barley, who looked up, wagging pleadingly until Micah looked down into Barley's anxious, upturned eyes and spoke. "Do you want to come home with us?"

Home.

It was a word Barley knew. And when Micah repeated it in his dog voice, Barley's joy let loose. He ran as fast as any dog had ever run—in circles! He dashed like a rabbit around Micah and his father, round and round, then stopped, reversed direction, and dashed madly around the other way as the Father scrambled for his walking stick and then for his coins. Micah pulled the knife from the ground and hurled it far into the roadside brush.

Micah helped his father raise up the cowl of his cloak to keep him warm, and the three of them started for home as the sky's last rays of pink faded to gray.

"We have to find a name for him," said Micah. "Though I suppose we could just call him Boy."

"No!" the father blurted. "We need something better than that."

"What?"

"I don't know," the father admitted. "I'll tell you what,"

he said to Micah, "tomorrow, after you get up and eat breakfast, take him for a walk over to the farm across the way
from our cottage. I imagine if you spend the day playing in
the fields and crops there, a good name will come to you."

"Speaking of eating, you must be famished, Father,"
said Micah.

"That I am."

"I have soup waiting for us at home."

"Soup sounds like just the thing."

"And bread. Our neighbor was worried about you. She
brought it by today for your return."

"Very kind of her," the old man said with a smile.

As they walked along, the father reached his hand down,
tousled the scruff on Barley's head, and said, "Are you going
to sit by the fire and have dinner with us, little one?"

"Remind me, Father—we'll need to get him a bowl."

The sun was just about to disappear over the road these
three were walking down. Early the next morning that
same sun would light the way of two women—friends of the
crucified man—as they went at dawn to the tomb of their
loved one to anoint his body with sweet oils, as was custom on the third day after death. But for now, the sun was
still a sliver of orange in the sky under which Barley and
his new master were heading home. Micah walked next to
his father, holding on to his arm as Barley trotted alongside

them both, walking and wagging, wagging and walking, but mostly wagging. He couldn't contain himself. Tomorrow would be Sunday, and Barley had a feeling it was going to be the best day ever.

DISCUSSION QUESTIONS

1. The story of Jesus's Passion has been called "the greatest story ever told." What are the elements of *plot*, *character*, and *theme* that have made this story so universal?

2. The epigraph of the book from the gospel of Matthew is about the good that comes to those who make sacrifices because of love. How does Barley's character arc exemplify this?

3. Barley, like all dogs, learns from his masters. What did he learn from Adah and Duv? And what are some of the harder lessons he learned from Samid?

4. It is Prisca who first sets Samid on his path to becoming "a good man." In what ways—both subtle and overt—does she do this?

5. The story is told primarily from Barley's perspective. How can looking at the story of Jesus's last days on earth through the eyes of a small, innocent creature bring new insights or resonances to this age-old story?

6. One of the major themes of the book is forgiveness. How does the power of *self*-forgiveness impact the characters in this book?

7. The setting of the book is Roman occupied first-century Judea. What do Barley and the other characters' tribulations tell us about the values of the world in which they live?

8. One of the few times Jesus speaks in the book he says, "For if people do these things when the tree is green, what will happen when it is dry?" What do you think Jesus means?

9. The question of what does or does not make someone a criminal is an important theme in the book and also a controversial issue in our own time. What relevance does Samid's plight have to the current conversation of the relationship between poverty, social marginalization, and incarceration?

10. Bread is one of the most powerful biblical metaphors of all. In *The Dog Who Was There* bread functions in both a metaphorical and a very literal way. What are the figurative and literal uses of bread in the book?

And what, in your own life, would you identify as your "daily bread"?

11. Many of us nowadays tend to greet our dogs more lovingly than we greet our family members and friends! Why do you think this is? What would happen if we treated each other in the same loving way we do our pets? What can we learn from animals about how to heal people with affection? (Animals can be healers. Have you ever seen the magic that a dog can work at a nursing home?)

ACKNOWLEDGMENTS

I must begin with endless thanks to Daniel Mallory whose wisdom and kindness were the wings that launched this project. My editor, Daisy Hutton, gave this book the gifts of her immense emotional intelligence and canny editorial instincts, and the team she has assembled at Thomas Nelson is all any writer could ask for. In my agent, Susan Schulman, I am blessed with a person of equal parts *heart, mind,* and *soul.* (And, let's be honest, there are some agents who are 0-for-3!)

I am so thankful to some of the early readers of this book whose faith in it made all the difference. Especially to my sister Karyn Gutierrez and to Nancy Blum whose handwritten note about this book has a special place on my shelf, as she and her husband Eddie have a special place in my heart. I am eternally grateful for Brian Shuff—and to his family whose cabin in Flagstaff is where the book began and a place of very happy memories. And I am thankful to playwright Beth Henley for her comments on the book and her irreplaceable friendship.

Other readers I wish to thank are Steve Rodriguez, my intrepid manager; Thom Ash, my first proofreader; publisher Greg Pierce of *ACTA*, a true mentor; and Nick Poehls, who is one of the smartest people I know.

I am indebted to my family for their interest in this work and their love for the "family eccentric" who wrote it. My parents are very devout, so their faith in this project meant the world. I am thankful to be one of six siblings who are all ardently supportive of each other, and I give special thanks to my sister Kathy for being both an official and unofficial coach throughout this process.

One of the secrets to being a writer is you have to have talented fiends. Marilyn Stasio has taught me more about writing than anyone I know. She is like a walking university—if universities smoked and said funny things. My years of discussing our mutual creative projects with Michael Goorjian makes me think of the Callimachus line:

"How often you and I had tired the sun with talking and sent him down the sky." And a champagne toast to Diane Benedict, with whom I once picnicked at Anton Chekhov's country house, and who has been a friend for all my working life.

There are a handful of special people at my university who mean a great deal to me. Judy Scalin, Joanne Connolly, Jason Sheppard, and Lane Bove are the very best of what it means to be an educator. And I am so thankful for April Rocha and Christopher Kelly, students in my first years of teaching who have become lifelong friends.

In closing, I want to give a special and, perhaps, unexpected thanks to the place where I first learned the sacred story at the heart of this book. I had no idea my early years at *Our Lady of Good Counsel* Grammar School in Washington Township, New Jersey, meant as much as they did until I wrote this book.

Finally, I wish to thank my dog Nelly who has been by my side through many years of work and life. (Nelly, I think one reason I wrote this book is to keep your light lit forever.)

ABOUT THE AUTHOR

 R on Marasco's first book *Notes to an Actor*, was named by the American Library Association an Outstanding Book of 2008. He cowrote the book *About Grief: Insights, Setbacks, Grace Notes, Taboos*, which has been translated into multiple languages. His most recent work is *Shakespeare: Portals to Prayer* and he is currently writing a book about Shakespeare's Sonnets. Ron has acted extensively on TV in everything from *Lost* to *West Wing* to *Entourage* and has done recurring roles

on *Freaks and Greeks* and *Major Crimes*. He appeared opposite screen legend Kirk Douglas in the movie *Illusion* for
which he cowrote the screenplay. He has a PhD in Theatre
History from UCLA and is a Professor at Loyola Marymount
University.